Published by stone circles, Durham, North Carolina.

Library of Congress Catalog Card Number: 99-76882
ISBN: 0-9672258-1-7

Cover design and layout by Ha Nguyen.

Katie Roiphe's essay, *A Grandmother's Biological Clock*, originally published
in the New York Times Magazine (February 8, 1998).

for my mom
and
the newest Hackett, soon to be born

Tema —

I hope these stories
might inspire something
unexpected + whimsical.
We — the young women in
the world — are so lucky to
have your wisdom + example
of courageous living. Enjoy! Maura

table of contents

acknowledgements

I would like to first acknowledge all of the women I interviewed who shared their stories and their time. This book is theirs and would not exist without them. Secondly, I want to thank the people all over the country who shared their homes, dinner tables, cars, computers and work spaces. You know who you are.

A host of organizations supported me while I did this project, they include: Do Something, The Bonner Foundation, Davidson College, Spontaneous Celebrations, Jumpstart, Youth on Board, and City Year. Individuals at all of these institutions provided critical feedback, support and joy that I will treasure always. The community of Mars Hill College not only allowed me to live and write for a semester on campus, they welcomed me into their world. Holly Blake and the WILL Program at the University of Richmond provided invaluable opportunities to test activities and exercises with their students.

There were a few advisors who supported my work abundantly and pushed me at critical moments. They include: Macky Alston, Mary Casey, Stan Dotson, Jean Entine, Cathy Jones, Nancy Kahan, Sandy Kaye and his writing class, Mel King, Fern Marks, Betty Powell, Ellen Porter Honnet, Firkins Reed, Amy Richards, Nancy Routh, Jeanette Shea and Juliette Zener.

I am grateful to my family for their support, especially my mom and sister, Katie, who motivated me to write this book. Jesse White, Wendy Root and Suzanne Hoffman provided incredible spiritual grounding. My friends made it possible for me to continue living through the moments when I was sure I would not make it: Claudia, Susan, Jenene, Jenny, Hez, Diane, Bobby, KP, Wayne, Julia, Brian, Maddy, Dana, JoAnne, Greg, Steph, Trudy, Ben, Katrina, and Tulaine. Arrington, my soul-sister for life, pushed and pulled at all the perfect moments.

Five people literally made the book a reality. Thanks to: Edith Buhs for endless hours of editing and support; Ned Rimer for being the best agent in the world; Ed Cohen for funding the printing; Ha Nguyen for a commitment to beauty and excellence in the graphics; and Meredith Weenick for skillfully editing and providing more patience than I could have imagined.

Without a higher power, none of this would have been possible.

introduction

I've been told that preachers preach what they need to hear and writers write what they need to read. I think there is a lot of truth to it.

Books have often been my best friends. Fresh out of college and living in Washington, D.C., when I couldn't find anyone to hang out with on a Friday night I turned to Natalie Goldberg, Alice Walker and May Sarton to keep me company. They were the best of companions—never too demanding, deeply moving, and always real. When I felt most isolated from the world, it was these women who reminded me that I was not the only one feeling this way. They connected me to a larger community where I felt accepted and sane. So at the end of my 20's, when I was struggling to make sense of the decisions I had made, it is not surprising that I ventured to write a book.

The fall after I turned 26 my life began a ride too wild for my own liking. Change met me at every crosswalk. In my early 20's I had flown around the country speaking to hundreds of people, challenging them to get involved in their communities. Now, I couldn't speak in front of ten people without my voice cracking. I left college with certainty that I would meet a man and get married. Now, I questioned the concept of marriage. In my teens, I was a Catholic lector. Now, I spent my mornings sitting on a meditation cushion in front of a picture of Sri Ramana Maharishi. I even began to question the motivation and logic behind the community organizing work I had done for almost a decade. Change was everywhere.

By the time I turned 28, a new set of questions floated in my mind. I wondered: Did I waste my 20's trying to save the world and forgetting to take care of myself? Could I follow a creative dream and pay the rent? Was is possible to be in a committed relationship and not lose myself? Part of my problem was the speed at which my life was moving. I wanted to slow down and be more thoughtful. I also wanted to learn from other people's choices. So I set out on a journey to find other women and listen to their stories.

I've always learned best by doing, and so I decided to write a book about the choices women make during their 20's. I interviewed women who were near my age, most of whom were between the ages of 25 and 35. I began with women who I admired and considered role models. Then I interviewed women I met as I traveled and others who were recommended. Finally, I turned to my close friends, many of whom had been my teachers for a long time. I knew the book would be biased by my interests, but I also tried to reach out to women to whom I wouldn't naturally be drawn.

I was surprised and excited by what I found. Woman after woman spilled forth her story. They spoke of major crises of faith; accidents that lead to a complete rethinking of their priorities; discoveries of sexual abuse that pushed them into a depression; break-ups that altered where they lived; and children that shook the core of their confidence. I was not alone. Women living in many different realities were entering their 20's and struggling to make decisions and find meaning, often in the midst of internal confusion and chaos.

Gail Sheehy, author of *Passages*, notes:

> The Trying Twenties confronts us with the question of how to take hold in the adult world. Our focus shifts from the internal turmoil of late adolescence—"Who am I? What is truth?"—and we become almost preoccupied with working out the externals. "How do I put my aspirations into effect?" "Where do I go?" "Who can help me?" "How did you do it?"
>
> In this period, which is longer and more stable compared with the passage that leads to it, the tasks are enormous as they are exhilarating: To shape a Dream, that vision of ourselves which will generate energy,

aliveness, and hope. To prepare for a lifework. To find a mentor if possible. And to form the capacity for intimacy, without losing in the process whatever consistency of self we have thus far mustered. (39)

Sheehy perfectly described my experience.

CONTRADICTING ISOLATION THROUGH STORYTELLING

On an August evening in the Puget Sound I sat across from Kristi, with her 2-week-old daughter snuggling into her chest. Listening to her story was one of the many gifts I took from this journey. For three hours she talked about having abortions, having babies, joining a spiritual community and struggling to tell the truth about her life to people around her. I listened and shared pieces of my story and realized how different, and how similar our stories were.

By the time I got up to go, we were both deeply moved by our time together. Through our stories, we affirmed each other's lives. I went back to my campsite that night and wrote for four hours, telling as much of the truth about myself as I could. The next morning, I felt a new energy and aliveness. Something about me had shifted: some layer of fear had left me that night. I was more ready to be myself. That is the power of storytelling.

In many cultures storytelling has a long, rich history. Telling stories has been a powerful way for people to pass down values, principles and information through the years. As the sound-bite age has gained ground, there is a greater need for storytelling in our daily lives. In 30 seconds you can report to your friends, "I am having a hard summer. My best friend moved and I'm feeling really lonely." But that does not get to the heart of the struggle. That brief report often misses the important details. With a cup of tea and an hour, a more detailed story might unfold. "I come home every night and make dinner for myself and get into bed and read, thinking that I can't believe I'm 29 and this is my life. I don't have a family, I work too much, and I am not really following my creative dreams. All summer I've worked in my garden to connect to the earth, but even that hasn't worked. I feel trapped in this city and long for the mountains and the ocean. I feel like I'm not really living my life and I am unsure about what to do about it. Up until now I've shifted small things around, and life's gotten better. Now I have the sense that something big needs to shift and I'm not sure what it is."

We all need to be witnessed and heard. We need people that welcome us to speak our truth and places where no one is watching the clock making sure we are not wasting time. We need more opportunities to examine the decisions we have made in the past, so that the ones we make in the future are more informed and grounded. And as much as we need to tell our own stories, we need to hear the stories of others.

One of the reasons why authors like Natalie Goldberg, Alice Walker and May Sarton have been so important to me is that I can relate to their stories. Something about their experience resonates inside of me. Their words have killed the storyline in my head that told me, "I'm the only one that has ever felt this way. I am crazy. I will feel this alone for the rest of my life." When I found the writing of author Annie Lamott, I loved her because she made fun of herself, and by laughing at her craziness, I could laugh at my own. It is this connectedness that many of us hunger for.

My hope is that this book will inspire women to share their stoires and create connections. Organized as a collection of stories of women and their choices, it highlights both their struggles and their victories.

As witnessing each of these stories changed me, I hope they will change you too.

THE JOURNEY OF 100 STORIES

The journey that began with interviewing a few role models in Boston continued through two years of travels that took me to Washington State, Oregon, Maine, North Carolina, Virginia, New York City, Boston and Yellow Springs, Ohio. In each place, I connected with people I knew, and people I didn't know.

I used no scientific process. I followed a mysterious path that led me from one woman to the next, never knowing where it would lead me. Interviews were taped on buses, trains, mountainsides, and city streets. Each woman interviewed offered anywhere from an hour to ten hours of her time to talk about decisions in her life. Each interview began with three primary questions:

- What are the three most significant decisions you've made since you've left school (however you define leaving school)?

- What did you learn from the decisions you made?

- Who and what are the people, places and things that influenced your decision making process?

The women whose stories follow are diverse in many ways. They have many different cultural backgrounds, lifestyles, types of work, family structures and educational backgrounds. Most are college educated. While several of the women interviewed grew up in poor families, most now consider themselves middle class.

As I look back I can see how who I am has greatly influenced the choice of stories. The process of creation was such a person journey that there is no way for the final product to be anything but biased by my interests, identity and struggles. I am an Irish/German, middle-class, Catholic woman who grew up in Old Tappan, New Jersey. I went to school at the University of Richmond, where I studied History and Women's Studies while spending most of my time doing community outreach work. Since graduation I have done youth and community organizing work all over the country. I am an artist at heart, and a mother-want-to-be. My commitment to my faith is what drives my life, and my curiosity about people is infinite.

As I interviewed women and reflected on their experiences, I questioned how differently these interviews might read if my population had been more diverse. I wondered what conversations might emerge if I had interviewed women without college educations, working poor, or women who had recently arrived in this country. It is likely that the economic and emotional pressures of poverty and immigration would limit the range of their choices. I have no way of knowing. I can only report that this is work left to be done.

There is something wonderful about knowing that this collection will never be done. It is a starting place. My hope is that it will inspire readers to share their stories and build this collection so that someday their is a library full of stories that people can access.

THE STRUCTURE OF THE BOOK

This book is divided into seven chapters. The first chapter focuses on my thoughts about the impact of speed, change and choice on this generation of young women. Chapters 2 through 6 focus on keys areas where women make decisions: Work; Sex, Children and Abortions; Depression, Addiction and Abuse; Relationships and Spirituality; and Art, Education and Adventure. The structure exists so that women looking for stories in a particular area can find them easily. In the introduction to each section, there is a short introduction to the topic and some of my experiences that relate to it. Each chapter leads with individual stories and ends with guiding questions and exercises. This book can be used as a guidebook or group discussion guide. The final chapter, "Just Lessons," outlines a few of the lessons I learned in writing this book.

Each story presented was created through a dialogue with each woman about her story. In some cases names are changed to preserve anonymity. The stories began as interviews that were transcribed and then shaped into case studies that were sent out and edited by the women I interviewed. Again they landed in my mailbox, either real or virtual, for final editing and adjustment. This process was a big part of the joy in making this book. Because we began with the spoken word, you may find some of the stories harder to read than you would a well-crafted essay. That is part of the beauty of the oral tradition—it is sometimes as imperfect as our lives.

Because one of the purposes of this book is to contradict isolation, the guiding questions and exercises sections were developed to assist groups of women in discussions about their lives. They can be used in academic settings, professional or personal retreats, informal dinner gatherings or workshops. Before you begin, consider finding a partner to read it with you.

ALLOWING SPACE FOR GRACE

If I had known when I started this project what it would take to finish, I might never have started. It is the most challenging thing I've ever done. This never would have been finished by sheer act of will alone. It took something beyond me to complete it. Persistence, patience and prayer are the disciplines that sustained me. In the final weeks of the editing I called a friend and explained that there was no way I could finish. Yet, I didn't want to disappoint all the women who had given so much of their time and stories, not to mention my friends who would kill me if I didn't finish it after so much talk and worry. She told me to hang on for a moment. When she returned, she instructed me to say "Now" when I was ready for her to pick a card. I waited a few seconds and said "Now." She paused and then read the word "grace" from a card. That was it. It was the perfect word. Grace was the only thing that would get me to the finish line.

Grace has gotten this book to you.

shifting ground

explore

tells you everything you need to know about her.
is doing well — how are you two? Have you sto.
yanking on his chains?
I was thinking today that this is such a
place to be — or would be if all of you were t
ently there's something called the Farmer's W
St every Saturday morning, which features t
near, produce from local farmer and the bu
markets will cook everything for you on the
might check me out next weekend, but hon
food isn't half as fun when you're not a
caroline to staff herself to the works along
The first thing I need to do this week is whip
some friends to have dinner with . . . one .
not working in a larger office is that my
own consists of a 40-something intellectual i

One Friday night while I was working on the final edits in this book, I left work and headed for the Kendall Cinema. It had been a hard day, and I needed an escape. A co-worker yelled at me for forgetting about a meeting, someone in my department quit, and for the third time in a week I hadn't had lunch until 3:00 p.m. I could feel the anxiety in my shoulders loosen as I parked the car. As I walked to the outside ticket window, I wondered if there was someone I could call to join me. I didn't feel like being alone. After I bought a ticket, I went inside and called my sister. I thought about calling another friend, but then decided against it. I walked back outside and sat on a bench and watched the sky in front of me turn from yellow to pink. A little voice in my head whispered, "You're just feeling lonely. Get up and do something about it."

It was a familiar voice. Sometimes I listened to it, sometimes not. This time I did. I walked back to the parking lot, got into my car and headed towards my friends' home in Central Square. Several times they had offered for me to join them for Shabbat, a Jewish ritual that takes place at sundown on Friday night, marking the start of the Jewish day of rest. As I headed down their street I felt shy for a moment. I wondered if I looked pathetic stopping by on a Friday night at diner time with no plans. People my age should be out on dates, with their friends at a party, or at home with families of their own. I pushed my worries aside and kept driving. Intuitively, something told me that I had to break the cycle of isolation that had left me depressed most of the summer.

A few minutes later I was at their front door facing Denis, with 3-month old Mia in his arms. "Hey, come on in," he bellowed in his large, deep voice. "Zoey, look who's here," he said to his 2 year-old daughter who was crouched on the floor playing with play dough. A big smile burst out on her face and she extended her hand with a piece of orange and green clay, a friendship offering. Zoey and I continued passing Play Doh back and forth while I explained to Denis that I stopped by just to say hello.

Within a few minutes Firkins, Denis's wife, joined us at the table and told me that I had to stay for dinner. Firkins set the table while Denis went to get the Shabbat candles. Then Firkins, Denis, Zoey and I joined hands, lit the candles, broke and ate bits of Challah bread, raised our wine glasses and sang the Shabbat prayers. Although I am not Jewish, I had heard the prayers enough in other settings to hum along.

After the ritual, we began talking about how too much of our lives were lived rushing around, feeling stressed and exhausted. It was a familiar conversation, that ended with our shared desires for life to slow down and be simpler. Eventually, the children were put to sleep and it was time for me to go. Warm hugs and promises to do this again were exchanged. I walked back to my car and before I turned the key I noticed the movie ticket sitting on the seat beside me.

That night it seemed that for a moment, I settled into myself. Rather than running to be entertained or to forget my loneliness, I turned towards the company of others, and it felt good. For 12 months during the writing of this book I had packed up and moved every couple of months. I was just begining to feel comfortable in my new apartment, but it was far from feeling like I had a home. Juggling both the writing of this book and my paid work left little time for settling in. I was exerting so much energy trying to keep up with the changes of the world around me, I was exhausted. This feeling was one I had become very familiar with during my 20's as the ground underneath me moved, and I struggled to regain my balance again and again.

When I left the movie theatre and headed for Central Square, I wasn't just looking for friends. I was seeking a place to rest. There were many friends I could have visited, but I chose Firkins and Denis. I knew their house was a place I could find a slower pace. Whenever I come by, things stop long enough for me to be noticed. They are rarely running out. Often they are home, feeding their kids, having conversations in the kitchen, or folding laundry. That night, I turned from my isolation and exhaustion to notice the abundance of connection around me. I explored a new reality, and in it I found great meaning.

It was yet another step in this journey in which something magical happened. By stepping back and taking a larger view, I learned exactly the lesson I needed to learn.

WHAT IS OUR WAR?

When I began writing this book a friend recommended that I speak to Mary Casey, a researcher at Harvard's Graduate School of Education. She had helped produce a book similar to mine twenty years ago. When we met, I described how I believed times had changed for women in the past twenty years, and explained that I was trying to capture some of the decisions and struggles that women are facing today. She listened and then began a string of questions about my research and topic: "Why are you interested in this topic? Why are there young people today turning 30 and acting as if they should have arrived at some great professional status?" Then she asked the question that remained with me all year: "What is the war your generation is fighting?" She explained, "In my generation, we were always wondering when the next bus was leaving to protest in Washington. We knew what we were fighting for."

As I left the meeting, the question stayed with me. I shared it in conversations at cocktail parties with my parents' friends, and at a St. Patrick Day's Parade with a stock broker. I raised it in conversations with my college roommates and in the dining hall at Antioch College with a group of students. I asked the question and listened to people's responses. And I tried out my answers too.

In her twenties, my mother's life was very different than mine. She did not have the time I do to sit around and think. She was busy taking care of the immediate needs of four children, a husband and a dying mother. There was a luxury of time I had in my life. I had new freedoms, but I wasn't sure they were all a good thing. There was some way in which I yearned for accountability. I could stay in bed on Saturday until noon. I could stay out dancing on a weeknight because I knew I could make up the sleep the next day after work. I could have men over all night without any worries of extended family members asking questions or giving me their words of judgment or concern. I was an independent woman in America, free to choose just about any lifestyle I fancied, with very few people to whom I had to answer. Yet, some of my choices left me feeling empty.

As I thought more about Mary Casey's question, I wondered if our struggle was connected to feeling connected and having meaning.

THE IMPACT OF FUTURE SHOCK

Not too long after my meeting with Mary, I decided to investigate other people's opinions about my generation. Until that point I had stayed away from popular opinions of Generation X, not wanting to be tainted by the stereotypes and psychological analysis of our problems. Somehow I ended up finding a book called *Future Shock*. At the time, I knew nothing about it. The title grabbed me so I flipped open the paperback's worn cover. It was written by a man named Alvin Toffler in 1977 about predictions for the future. The book made a very convincing argument that the technology age would bring about change so rapidly that there would be an epidemic of "future shock." As Toffler describes, future shock is "the distress, both physical and psychological, that arises from an overload of the human organism's physical adaptive systems and its decision-making processes." (326) Future shock would be characterized by a rise in depression, alcoholism, violence, and confusion. Toffler, along with his predictions, notes that:

> We have not merely extended the scope and scale of change, we have radically altered its pace. We have in our time released a totally new social force—a stream of change so accelerated that it influences our sense of time, revolutionizes the tempo of our daily life, and affects the very way we "feel" the world around us. (17)

As I read on, many things in the book rang true. I definitely felt that my life was often spinning around me. Many women I talked to described considerable distress that resulted from all of the changes in their lives. One of my friends told me she had moved 20 times in her life as she sat crying over a painting that had been destroyed in a flood. It was one of the only things she owned that connected her to her past. Another woman profiled in this book packed her bags and re-settled every year between the ages of 16 and 30. At 30, she decided enough was enough and bought a house so that she could control her living situation. A colleague on the phone one day said "I'm not sure where I am." She had eaten breakfast in North Carolina, lunch in Boston and dinner in Chicago. Movement and change for many of us is too familiar. And it is not just physical. There is also shifting on an emotional and spiritual level. Many of us feel secure and sure of ourselves one day and completely lost the next. Just as we think the situation we are in has stabilized, we look down and there is new ground beneath our feet. Our environment is rapidly shifting and there is little that we have to help us remain balanced.

Whether it is future shock, impermanence or chaos—many of us are feeling the effects of a world in which change is happening faster than we can adapt. Laura, interviewed in the book, confirms that symptoms of future shock are all around us. At the end of her interview she stated sadly:

We're not connected to things anymore. We get in our cars, we eat out in restaurants, we send letters to people without even lifting a pen. There is very little process to our lives. We can buy everything from dinner to houses—ready made. You don't learn how to do things for yourself, and you're not a part of the process of creating.

NEW CHOICES

In addition to pace and change, we are also faced with many new options. As women, our choice of work, lifestyle, family structure and more has changed dramatically in the past twenty years. While there is great excitement and opportunity with these options, they also can be confusing and overwhelming. Several mothers of 20 year-olds I talked to spoke about how challenged their children seemed over decisions that they had never considered. One told her daughter, "If I had thought as much about marrying your father as you are about marrying your boyfriend, I never would have done it." Another observed, "My daughter gets caught and overwhelmed by the multitude of decisions before her, it makes me recognize that there are some downsides to all of this choice we have worked so hard for your generation to have."

While our choices have increased, we are also less grounded in principles and values that help us make decisions. Ellen, one of my advisors on this book, discussed this with me over lunch one day. I explained that I believed that my generation was caught in an in-between stage. It felt as though we were placed in a candy store and whoever was tending the store went outside and said to us, "Do whatever you want in here until I get back." So, here we are, doing whatever we want and feeling really confused about what we should be doing and what we shouldn't be doing. Some think it is fine to eat whatever is on the shelf and others think it is wrong. Some of us sit on the candy counter, and others are horrified by the counter-sitters, but don't want to interfere. We are each doing our own thing, not taking responsibility for the entire store, and somewhat unclear if what we are doing is acceptable or not.

Ellen responded by saying, "The groundrules used to be clear. Norms were set, and if you went against them, there were ramifications. As people resisted choices being dictated for them, the groundrules began to shift. As our freedom of choice has expanded, I wonder if our decisions are as clearly grounded in values as they used to be. Freedom without responsibility can result in chaos."

Teaching second grade confirmed for me the critical need for groundrules. I wasn't used to taking a firm stand on what is acceptable, and what is not acceptable and the kids knew it. In three short weeks they walked all over me as I struggled to set rules and keep them accountable. Taking a firm stand was counter-intuitive. Working with teens, I had gotten used to allowing young people to lead and supporting them as they worked towards their dreams. I was not experienced with the idea that varying levels of freedom correspond with different levels of responsibility. So when I found myself as the authority figure in front of a class full of 7 and 8 year-olds, I was in a foreign land. I had very little practice being a directive leader. The only way I was going to get Louis to stop hitting Ralph was by being clear about what is acceptable and what is not, and holding them accountable to the class rules. It was a major challenge to my way of being. As I moved into my fourth week, I was learning. I began to notice that the kids wanted and needed this firmness. They wanted an orderly and safe classroom. Limiting their choices wasn't such a bad thing.

The isolation and exhaustion I felt that night in Central Square and often during my 20's was closely linked to these new choices. Perhaps it was the combination of so many choices and the message of, "Do whatever you want to do," that has resulted in a feeling of overwhelm. I spent many hours during my 20's contemplating my choices. What did I want to do with my life? Where did I want to live? Did I want to work full or part time? Should I wait until I have money to buy a car, or should I take out a loan? What about graduate school? With whom do I want to live my life?

Toffler predicted that so many choices would contribute to a sense of apathy and deep withdrawal:

> The confusion and uncertainty wrought by transience, novelty and diversity may explain the profound apathy that de-socializes millions, old and young alike. This is not the studied, temporary withdrawal of the sensible person who needs to unwind or slow down before coping with his problems. It is total surrender before the strain of decision-making in conditions of uncertainty and overchoice. (363)

That we struggle to make meaning is also linked to the challenge of overchoice. It is easy, when then you are overwhelmed by choice, to check out or give up. Clarity can seem distant or impossible. And the pace of our lives is not conducive to slowing down and hearing the deeper yearnings of our heart. As I returned again to Mary Casey's question, I began to consider the possibility that our consciousness is under attack. The speed, the choices, the lack of grounding all makes it challenging for us to be thoughtful and clear about our choices, to care deeply about the world, or to take bold stands on issues. I was beginning to believe that there is a subtle, but powerful, assault on our consciousness.

There are many women, however, who rise above this assault, think carefully about their decisions and engage deeply with the world. Ruth, an interviewee explained her theory while we sat in the back of her Portland, Oregon, home:

> "I think we have reached the end of the Age of Exploration. There are no more frontiers. People keep trying to create them but it is an artificial sense of limits and boundaries. What is challenging is everyday. Finding ways to live day to day gracefully. People might think making change means inventing something new or bringing economic progress to the third world, but I don't see it that way. I see that everyone needs to pick up their trash consistently. Everyone needs to figure out ways to use a little bit less stuff and to value what we have."

If nothing else, it was becoming very clear that new choices have given us new freedoms and new burdens.

OUR RELATIONSHIP TO SACRIFICE

One of the first places I stayed for an extended period of time during my research was my parents' house in the Berkshires, where I joined my mom, dad and 93 year-old aunt. One day over a sandwich we began talking about war. My dad and aunt reminisced about growing up. My dad spoke of the air raids and sugar rations during World War II. They talked about my uncle who left a young man in his late twenties and returned with a full head of white hair. He never once talked about his experiences of fighting. As they talked I thought about the many young people who never returned. They sacrificed their lives, children, and material goods for the sake of the country.

Listening to my dad and aunt made me realize how little I know of sustained sacrifice. There hasn't been any war that has felt real to me. Watching the U.S. bomb Iraq or Kosovo was like watching a movie. In terms of my daily life, if I have to sacrifice too much, I attempt to get out of the situation. If I don't like my job, I quit. If a relationship gets hard, the first place my mind goes is to consider leaving. My desire for comfort fights with my desire for courage. In part this may be a normal human response, but I think it is heightened because of the avoidance-of-pain mentality by which I have been surrounded.

Later in my journey I moved to the tiny mountain town of Mars Hill, North Carolina. At a focus group I convened of women of many different ages, this topic arose. This time it focused on my generation's preoccupation with pleasure and immediate gratification. Many women there remarked that we have been raised on TV, which gives us what we want when we want it. Tisha, the youngest woman present that night, who is in her early 20's, confirmed the older women's thinking. "Just about everything I do is based on immediate gratification. It is what I want right now, not what I need to have in the long run. Up until this year, everything I did was because I wanted an instant outcome, not ten minutes from now or an hour from now."

INSTITUTIONS AND MEANING

One of the reasons the evening I spent in Denis and Firkin's home was so meaningful was that it was grounded in family and in faith. As we lit the Shabbat candles and we all joined hands, even 2 year old Zoey sang the words she knew. We broke bread and drank wine in the same way and at the same time that many other households were doing all over the world. We enacted a ritual that Denis's parents and grandparents and great grandparents had done on Friday nights throughout their lives. Through this ritual, we were passing on a piece of the Jewish tradition and connecting to the past, present and future.

Unfortunately, not everyone is fortunate to have rituals like this one in their lives. Susan, one women interviewed, grew up with parents who had both left the church. She told me with frustration:

> "I grew up with nothing—we didn't go to church or read the Bible. I always found religion scary and confusing. My mom grew up in a really strict Catholic home and my dad was Episcopalian but by the time I was born, neither believed in religion any more. God was considered a bad word in my house."

A week later I interviewed a parent who talked about her 20-year-old daughters being good Jewish women if they simply made it to synagogue on the Jewish holidays. Both of these conversations made me question the impact of alienation and distance from the institutions of family and religion.

Family, as an institution, plays a very different role in many people's lives today. Not only has the divorce rate skyrocketed, many parents play a less significant role in rule making. In my work with teens I once mediated a conversation between a teen-age woman and her mother. The mother, new to this country, was horrified that her child was not living according to the family's rules. The daughter, having spent several years in American schools, was fighting to be respected as an individual, capable of making her own rules. Angie, another interviewee, added some perspective on the shifting institutions, such as family, in our lives, "I think we are the first generation of people to feel really comfortable leaving our families and the areas that they come from. I'm from Iowa. There has never been anyone in my family that has said, OK, I'm going north, or I'm going to the city. But I didn't think twice about it."

There was a power in the Shabbat blessing and the lifting of the cup. It was a ritual that helped to preserve a set of values that has been passed down from generation to generation. And both family and religion played an important role in maintaining it.

EXPLORING REALITIES

That night with Denis and Firkins, I was reminded again that the possibility of meaning lies in everything. It's not what I do that matters, it is how I do it. The important questions are: Are we moving slowly enough to realize where and how we are? Are we connected enough to our spirit and our souls to feel something deeper than the surface level? Are we allowing ourselves to be vulnerable and changed by our relationships and the world?

Reversing disconnection and meaninglessness is not easy work. Neither is combating the assault on our consciousness. It takes the same slow toil of a gardener turning the soil, daily attending to the weeds, the quality of the dirt and the health of the plants. Day after day being present. Noticing where we get dull, cut off, numbed-out or disconnected. Noting when we are energized, connected and full will help us to know when to till and when to plant. This vigilance will inform our decisions so that through our realities, we find meaning.

Despite the unique challenges of our generation, I was struck by the courage and creativity of the women interviewed. Many women I met didn't step a beat before they did something their mothers never dreamt of doing. Most of the women I interviewed are creating bold lives in the midst of confusing times. Although some of them went through trying times of confusion and lack of confidence somewhere along the way, many of them made it through the storm stronger than ever. They were not limited by the picture they saw painted for them by someone else.

My hope is that this book sparks a conversation about the trends I observed. Do they resonate with you? How are pace and choice impacting our lives? Do we need to be training young people to better adapt to change? Do we need to help people think about a new relationship to pain and sacrifice? Do we need new institutions or do we need to re-invest in the old institutions of family and religion?

As you read about the decisions women have made concerning work, sex, children, abortion, depression, addiction, abuse, relationships, spirituality, art, education and adventure, you may see, as I have, the evidence that many in their 20's and 30's feel as though the ground is shifting underneath them. Each woman speaks of her own journey to find more stable ground and to create a life with meaning. I hope that as you read these stories you will reflect on your decisions and the consciousness that you bring to your life as you explore your reality.

choosing work

explore

When I graduated from college I didn't know what I was going to do next. I worked for my dad's tree service company for a few weeks before I got a job helping to start a foundation in Washington, D.C. For two years my work was my life, as I traveled around the country talking to young people and community leaders. At the end of the two years I was sick and burnt out. Work had not served me well. It dominated too much of my life and left little time to cultivate my relationships and my spirit. I made my next move in order to follow a relationship, not a job. When I did settle into a job, I attempted to have more balance in my life, which I'm sure helped me work more effectively. I started a nonprofit which gave me more flexibility. At the end of four years, I again felt burnt out and a lack of balance between my work and personal life. I decided it was time to follow a dream, to take a risk and so I made the choice to write this book. I now have a new appreciation of how fulfilling work can be. Rather than viewing work as something that merely drains me, I now see it as a part of my life that can give me energy and excitement. I expect the balance challenge will always be one I struggle with, but at least now I have a new concept of how it can be different.

Choosing where to work, defining why you work, and creating a way to work takes a tremendous amount of thought and energy for most people. The choices we make about work can have a dramatic impact on our life. Taking a job in San Francisco when you live in Washington, D.C., requires that you to turn most of your life upside-down. A new mom deciding to take a job outside the home will also require major changes. Many college students looking ahead to their future get mentally and emotionally paralyzed by the idea of having to choose what they will "do" with their life. Twenty years ago most women looked at their job possibilities and saw five options: secretary, teacher, nurse, housekeeper, or mother. Women today can choose just about any work, from pilot to investment banker to entrepreneur to minister.

The good news about this changed climate is that it creates more lifestyle options. More companies are developing policies that allow employees to work from home, job share, or have their children cared for at their workplace. More young people are able to create the job of their choice, rather than join a corporate giant and become one more cog in the wheel. With this increase in choices comes the challenging task of navigating through the options.

Another factor in this changing world of work is that we no longer have to choose a job for life. In fact, it would be difficult to do that if we tried. The Bureau of Labor Statistics reports that, "Most young people today will go through at least seven job changes in their lifetime." We are also a part of a generation that is starting its own businesses and nonprofits at a much higher rate than in the past. Women-owned businesses are one of the fastest growing segments of our economy; they are starting at twice the rate of their male counterparts. Sixty-four percent of women between the ages of 18 and 34 say they want to be business owners.(SBA database) It is clear that the landscape for women's work has changed dramatically in the past 20 years. What is not so clear, and what poses one of this generation's greatest challenges, is how to keep up with it.

In *She Works / He Works*, Rosalinda Barnett and Caryl Rivers note that:
> We may have seen the end of work as we once knew it – a linear progression through one company, a journey taken mainly by men, who are rewarded for good work by job stability and continuing rises in the level of pay. We have to examine a whole range of new ideas – flextime, compressed days, flexible hours, more use of electronic technology to replace some face time at work. (239)

Hearing each of the following women's stories, I thought about different elements of choosing, sticking with, or leaving work situations. They reminded me how complex work-related decisions can be, and how important they can be to living a good life.

- Tene reminded me that going after a dream takes a tremendous amount of persistence and risk taking. Her description of setting herself up in the right school to get the right internships so that she would have the experience she needed, took a tremendous amount of focus and discipline. When she told me about asking her boss if she could co-host a TV production after only 2 months on the job, she reminded me how rewarding taking a risk can be and how if you are going to be in a public job, you can't take things personally.

- Not everyone has the courage or opportunity to follow a dream. Gretchen did, and her story is an inspiring one. She learned a lot when she set out to start an Internet cafe with her husband and some friends. But now, when people ask her the magic in doing it, her challenge to them is "to figure it out for yourself."

- "Go for it." That's what Laura would say to any woman who is thinking about moving into another job or a different field. By getting an internship in a publishing house, while holding down her paper-pushing job, she moved herself right around the block, and into a new field of work.

- Angie spoke of the challenge and creativity required in doing art and doing work that sustains the physical needs of your life. She describes not only what her path was, but also some of the influences along the way. She challenges us to look at our dartboard – who is it that we allow to influence us when we are making decisions? Are they the right people or people we are accustomed to being influenced by?

- Deborah talks about navigating a challenging work situation and the value in having others around as role models and advisors.

- Maria and Rachel offer insight into the corporate world as women, and the challenges that can arise in a man's world.

- Every job is not an open door for a woman. I almost forgot that until Kim's story reminded me of it. She had to be creative and steadfast in her desire to pursue pastoral ministry. She brings forward issues related to working in partnership with a significant other and moving through the trap of pleasing people in a job context.

tene

Tene, 27, grew up in several Atlanta suburbs, went to Davidson College and then landed in Charlotte, North Carolina, working in television as a public affairs assistant. She now runs her own weekly talk show. She is African-American, single and an active member of a Presbyterian church.

When I met Tene at the TV station in Charlotte I didn't know what to expect. After a short wait she greeted me and escorted me back to the filming studio. We sat in two chairs up on the stage, as if we were being filmed for one of her shows. Big lights hung down in front of us and camera stands hovered a few yards away. As I listened to her talk I had the feeling I was sitting with one of the "soon to be famous" people in our generation.

Tene's poise, honesty and clarity inspired me to reflect on what I wanted to become excellent at in my lifetime. It was clear that she was following a calling, and her passion made me think about what I was called to do. She had obviously set her mind on becoming great at TV production. As new doors have opened for women in the professional world, TV production is definitely an area where new territory has been charted by women in the past 20 years. Tene made me wonder what's ahead, and what it will take women to get there.

TENE'S STORY

I knew all along, even before I went to college that I wanted to have my own production company and my own TV show so I could do what I wanted without having the network tell me what I could do. Oprah is a great example of what I want. But she didn't really have any power until she created Harpo, her own company. Before creating her own company she was working in public affairs in Chicago. There are always certain restrictions when you work for someone else: you can't say certain things and you always have that little message at the end of the show that says "the views of this show do not necessarily reflect the views of this station." If you have your own company, you can say and do what you want, as proven by Oprah's court case. So that was my goal. I figured by going to Davidson College I could get a good start.

With a major in psychology, everyone always asks me, how did you end up here (with my own TV show)? When I chose a college I knew Davidson was a liberal arts school and that they didn't have a journalism or TV studies program, but I knew I could get really good internships through the school. In my freshman year I started doing an internship back home in Atlanta with the NBC affiliate where I worked each summer. That's how I got my real experience. I figured I could major in anything when my boss in Atlanta told me, "Do not major in communication or journalism; there are too many people with worthless degrees, so do not major in these areas. Major in something like economics or psychology, something specific but broad, and then if you want to go to graduate school, you go." She said I wouldn't use a communications degree, and she was right.

My job title now is public affairs assistant. I am responsible for producing a public affairs show, which sounds fancy but includes a lot of mundane work. I took the job realizing that it might not be a good fit for me, but also knowing that I needed to get my foot in the door. It's been the best thing for me.

On my first day at the station I cried because the environment was so hard. My boss didn't have many social skills. He showed me to my cubicle and said, "You need to produce some new shows," knowing full well that I had no production experience. I wanted him to give me a little direction, to sit me down and tell me what they wanted, and how they had it done in the past. There was none of that. He just left me there on my own.

I started getting people to come on the show. After I had been producing the program for two months, I asked my boss if I could host it. He said, "I don't care, do what you want to do." So I did; I hosted my own show.

I loved doing the show but knew I needed to learn a lot. I never had anyone to sit down and talk it through with. Still, I was comfortable in front of the cameras and talking with people about whatever I wanted. By far the two most interesting shows I've hosted were ones on homeless awareness and battered women. For the homeless awareness show, I planned to interview two people – a single mom with three kids and a popular DJ in Charlotte who had been homeless. We were on the set, all ready to go, but the DJ didn't show. So it was just me and this woman. It was the most intimate interview I had ever done. The woman talked about being homeless and her baby getting sick, and where people could go for help. Sometime after this interview, I got a phone call from a guy who said, "Ma'am, I didn't remember the station you worked for but I remembered your name, and I called around to all the stations trying to find you. I'm a sales person and I didn't get my commission check, and I think my children are about to be homeless. Can you give me that number that you gave on your show?"

I was on cloud nine after that call, because I felt like I was changing people's lives. The show comes on so early that I never think anyone really watches, so when he called me, I got chills up my arms. I will probably never see or meet him, but he helped me see I did something that mattered.

I did another show with a woman who had been beaten by her partner for several years. As she was telling her story, she was on the verge of tears the whole time. At the end of the show, I just started to cry. All of my co-workers were thinking, "Oprah moment, oh God!" I ended the show with my voice cracking. Her story really touched me.

Being in this industry is not easy. I'm in it because I think it is truly my life calling, what I am meant to do. I believe in divine order, and I believe this is where I am meant to be. But it was hard to get in. I had to work two summers for free so I could get the exposure and be able to put on my resume, "NBC affiliate in Atlanta."

To succeed in this business you really need to network, to know people. You should have an idea where you want to be geographically and start networking early on in that area. My job is the lowest of the low, but it is giving me exposure and experience. I could easily be doing behind-the-scene work, but I knew if I wanted to be in front of the cameras, I had to take risks. I took the risk by having the guts to go to my boss after being here only three months and say, "Hey, I think I look better than our current host. Can I be in front of the cameras? Take a look, let me do one show, and if you don't like it I won't do it anymore. But if you do like it, then let me continue to do it." If he had said no I would have gone back again a month later.

There are a lot of big egos in this industry. A lot of people aren't making much money, so they are being fed by the power of someone saying, "This is what we're going to put on the air," or "This is what we are going to promote." If people perceive that you are somehow messing with their power, they get very upset and angry with you.

I've learned not to take things personally. My first month here was hard because I had come from a very sheltered environment. When I worked at Davidson and didn't feel well, people would say, "Take a vacation, just relax." This industry is not like that at all. You could be on your deathbed, and you are expected to come to work. You learn that it has nothing to do with you. It's about getting the job done. I've learned that's how these people are and I need to accept them as they are. I hope they change, but if they don't I still have to get my job done. It's a bit of a joke how clear I am with people at work. I tell them, "I'm not here for you to like me. You hired me to do a job, and I need some assistance to do it. Let's just get it done." I have worked hard to advocate for support for myself and to learn not to take criticism too personally.

Another area at work that has been important is my image. It's important in part because I'm black, and I always feel that I need to look better because of it. It's also important because of the nature of the job. After the first time I was on camera my colleague sat down with me and said, "You need to get rid of the mustache. Just put some Nair on it." I thought, what? Now I have to take care of that every month. Do you know how much that costs? But he had to be blunt with me because on camera it's all about image and how you show up. He said, "You need to get some new makeup and cover those blemishes." I just had to accept it. I told him later I went home that day almost in tears. I thought I was a decent looking person until that day.

I go to jazzercise three times a week, I drink a whole bunch of water, and I'm blessed because I don't really gain weight. I now have to get my hair done more regularly. Before being in this career I could not have cared less about it. I could put on my Daisy Dukes cut-off shorts and a tee-shirt and go to the grocery store and it wasn't a big deal. But after the first time someone recognized me, I realized that image is everything. I wear my contacts all the time now, even though I used to wear my glasses if my eyes were tired.

This job has taught me, on a lot of levels, not to take things personally. There is just a lot I have to accept if I'm going to do the job right.

gretchen

Gretchen is 33, white and married. She was born and still lives in Seattle. She runs an internet service provider and Internet cafe with her husband and friends called the Speakeasy and is an artist of many forms.

I waited to meet her sitting at the counter at the Speakeasy and looked around. There were a group of friends drinking coffee next to a big window lining the street and several individuals sitting at computers pounding away on the keyboards in a different section of the room. A cute guy behind the counter asked me if I wanted anything to drink. I was in my wonderland. I was sitting inside the cafe I had once dreamt of creating.

An hour later I sat across from Gretchen on a black metal folding chair in the performance space in the back of the cafe. I was inspired even further. Gretchen made me think about what it takes to follow a dream, and what rewards are possible if you do. She reminded me of the choice of many in our generation to give up traditional career paths and launch new businesses or non-profits. Her challenge to "figure it out for yourself" reminded me that we each have our own path and it's our job to figure out what it will be.

GRETCHEN'S STORY

When I got out of school I knew I didn't want to go work for somebody. I also made the decision not to go into clothing design, even though that's what I had studied. I had always been poor and doing clothing design meant I would stay poor. Generally, no one makes money unless you make it really big. The industry is filled with sweatshops, even here in Seattle. I worked at a company as a freelance pattern maker, and the owner couldn't communicate with his workers and treated them poorly. I thought, wow, this is a really bad industry. I wasn't sure how I could affect it.

When my husband Michael got a company cash bonus for an idea he had, he could have moved right up the corporate ladder. We decided since we had some money and people to support us, we'd go for our dream. Michael and I had been living with an eclectic group of people in an old unfurnished warehouse. We were always throwing around idea of starting a cafe because of the community we enjoyed there. We had friends who were actors and writers who wanted to open a theater. My husband was into computers and had just discovered the Internet. So, we rented the space and created Speakeasy—an "Internet cafe" with theater in the back, politics debated out front, and space for visual artists to show their work. We created it with a lot of sweat and ideas and very little money. The chairs and tables were made from 2x4's and 2x6's my husband's father donated. All of the kitchen equipment we found second hand. With a six-inch disk sander we ground off the paint to expose the beautiful wood beams and repainted the walls with boneyard paint we mixed into colors with pigments.

At the cafe we try to facilitate events our clients are interested in, including fundraisers, political events, book signings, and speakers. We try to curate the space and avoid renting it out like a hall. We have music out front, which we always try to make ambient, so it sets an atmosphere where you can sit down and work. Planned Parenthood set up a booth here one night. It is funny how people come to you. We don't seek out too much, but there aren't that many avenues for people to show their work, hold small performances or do community events. When people ask what it takes to do something like this I usually won't talk to them. The first thing they need to learn is that you've got to figure it out yourself.

If you go into business with someone you should know what their motive is. Some people go into business because it is a life choice they've made and they want to be very involved with it. Other people go into business wanting to get rich quick. You have to be careful of that type. You don't need to sacrifice your whole life for your business, but you will have to sacrifice a big section of your life for some time. That commitment tests you. Your integrity is tested all the time in business.

People say don't go into business with your friends or family, yet I've done it all. Michael and I always spent a lot of time together, so we already knew we would do fine. We've gotten to know each other better through the experience. I know he gets stressed out when it comes to money. When his stress level goes up I have to be cool about it. The toughest times have been the most rewarding. Everything in life is a big learning process. Starting a business is no different.

laura

Laura is 27 years old, single, white and living in Seattle. She grew up in Michigan where she attended Michigan State University and majored in English. Since graduating, she has bagged groceries, made pizzas, pulled espresso, waited on tables, bartended and voiced on-hold phone messages. She is currently the Assistant Editor of the Best Places guidebook series at Sasquatch Books. She also writes, snowboards, plays soccer and dodges cars on her bicycle commute.

Laura and I met for this interview in a small cafe a short distance from her job. She came in off a bike, helmet in hand and rapidly reclined in a big chair by the window. I had just put down my journal, writing about how great life seemed out on the west coast. Because she was in the publishing world I was excited to both interview he, and get her insight on moving this project into published form. In just an hour she spilled out her story and lots of great publishing tips.

Her story reminded me of the impact of dislocation on our generation. She, like many, has moved far away from her family. She also challenged me to think about putting something other than work as a priority in choosing a place to live. The piece of her story that most inspired me was her initiative and creativity in moving from one job to another. She was another woman who was ignoring norms of the work world and forging a path of her own.

LAURA'S STORY

One of the first major decisions I made in my twenties was to move away from the place where I had grown up for twenty-two years. I knew I needed to go someplace new. I moved to Colorado with two friends – to Boulder – because we wanted to be near the mountains. It was a bit chaotic. I worked three places in three months and I had no money, but I had an adventure every day. We went to festivals and did a lot of hiking, biking, and running. I was healthier than I've ever been because I wasn't buying anything I didn't need. I ended up working in a coffee shop and a pizza place, having a really good time.

I left Colorado two years later, after I had bartended and been a ski bum in Steamboat Springs. I loved it there, but I knew at a certain point that it was time to leave. I didn't want to own a bar or a resturant. I wanted more diversity, more culture, more music. I knew I needed to be somewhere different.

I decided to move to Seattle and try to start a career. It seemed like an easy decision, but it was monumental because I was completely changing my lifestyle. I was used to having a lot of free time in Steamboat. All of the sudden I was a slave to an office for at least eight hours a day. When I first moved to Seattle, I was selling tickets at the Monorail, a job I'd taken just to make ends meet and planned on working for only a couple of weeks. My friend had been working for a company who needed a temp for two months, and she asked me if I was interested. I said yes, thinking, "Of course I'll try the temp job, even though I've never worked full time in an office. It can't be that different, right?" What I assumed would be a short-term position turned into two years at a paper-pushing office job.

A year ago, I said to myself, "I am so unhappy at this job. I've got to do something to change it." I'd been sending out resumes, but nothing was happening —my experience wasn't unusual, nothing made me stand out. I went through a tough time where life was hard, and I was searching for meaning. It was really rainy. I hated my job and I thought, "Why am I here?" I needed to examine my situation because there were a lot of negative elements in my life at that point.

I realized that I was frustrated where I was working. I knew there must be more rewarding jobs. While I was re-evaluating my resolve to change, I happened to read three essays in *Ms. Magazine* that were reprinted from a Seal Press book, *Listen Up: Voices From the Next Feminist Generation*. In the back of my mind, I remembered an internship at Seal Press that I had heard about when I first moved to Seattle. I knew that I could juggle my existing full-time job with a part-time (eight hour) internship. So I talked to my manager and my boss and they agreed to let me pursue the opportunity. I thought, "Sure, I'll be busier, but *who cares*?"

I went to my internship at Seal Press two afternoons a week. On those days, I arrived at 7:00 a.m. at my full-time job and left at 1:00 p.m. I worked at Seal from 1:00 to 5:00 p.m. The businesses were only a couple blocks apart, so it was easy to get from one to the other. The rest of the week I worked 7:30 a.m. to 4:30 p.m. My boss was understanding, and flexible about my hours. The days were long but I loved it. Eventually it led to a full-time job at Seal Press.

The realization came to me a couple of months ago that I'm probably not going to make a lot of money in my life. I don't want to work in sales. Non-profit work and small businesses are what I care about. It's a choice that many people have to make – make money or pursue a labor of love – and my decision is that I would rather like what I do.

If other women are thinking about doing something like this, I say, "Go for it!" It's never too late. Think about what your interests are and talk with your current boss about flexible hours. Ask people who you want to work with if you can intern, or volunteer at night or on the weekends to gain exposure to a field. If it's important enough for you to leave your current job, it's worth it to work the longer hours.

For me, I didn't want to leave my job just for a little more money. I wanted to do something that I really care about.

angie

Angie, 30, is a chef and an artist. She is a white woman who lives with her partner in Seattle after moving, almost overnight, from a small town in Iowa where she grew up. Angie graduated from the University of Iowa where she studied painting. She is finally learning how to surf and is really glad that during her 20's she played drums with a punk band.

She was my final interview in Seattle and by the time we met I was already convinced that Seattle was a place full of inspiring women. We met at yet another one of the city's cafe/bookstores. This one sold homemade Ring Dings and had tables out on the street where we sat as we talked. After the interview we moved to a bar across the street with the woman who had told me to call Angie and celebrated a final farewell to the city before my flight home.

Angie challenged me to think about work and art, and how the two can go together. She also was a welcome challenge to the notion that money and things should be the focus of so much attention. She articulated what many in our generation are acting out—a desire to create a good life above and beyond the most profitable work. While she talked about the people that influence our decisions, the interview also made me think about the larger trends that influence us without our being aware of them.

ANGIE'S STORY

I've been conditioned all my life to make money to buy a house and car and other things. But I've been around long enough to see that it hasn't brought me much happiness.

After college I had no idea what to do. There are not that many options for someone who got a degree in painting. I moved to Colorado and then to Seattle. When I arrived in Seattle I had only $500 and all of my stuff. I got my first cooking job when I bumped into a place looking for someone to do dishes and cut up vegetables. I wasn't even qualified for it. I had been making mayonnaise and tuna salad at my last job, but I put on my resume that I had experience in several culinary arts. I got the job and cooked there for two years before I decided that it was time to go.

I started cooking for money so that I could paint, but ever since I started I've found so many similarities between cooking and painting. My challenge has been finding the balance between the two. At 25, I had been cooking for two years and decided I would quit to paint more. I took up a job I thought I could lay back in so I could paint, and instead I ended up as the lead chef.

The first chef I worked for in Colorado told me he gave up painting for food and now cooking is what he does as art. At the time I thought that was such a cop out, but now I really see how cooking can become just as much an art form as painting. At work I try to come up with specials, and it becomes a big fusion of flavors. I get home and begin to paint and pretty soon it becomes a fusion of colors. It's similar and yet very different at the same time. There are a lot of people who do both.

I don't know how responsible I've been for these decisions; it's just where I have been led. I made the decision to quit jobs simply because I knew that I had to go. There is an alarm that goes off when I start getting bored. I start getting lazy, and when I start feeling that in a job, I have to go.

Some people stay in jobs because they are petrified. They start feeling tired, getting grumpy, and feeling lethargic because they are bored. It takes so much bravery to leave a job, but the freedom feels really good.

The hardest part of my lifestyle has been dealing with my family, who is constantly saying, "Why don't you go to Boeing or get a job at Microsoft and work with computers?" I have to keep telling my mom I just don't want to do that. I can't sit down for that long. My family doesn't get the idea of working for a while and then taking six months off to paint, or of having non-traditional hours. They have worked 9 to 5 all of their lives. I struggle to justify my existence to my family who just doesn't get it. At some point you have to say, "You're not going to get it and that's OK," and then decide where they are going to be in your life.

I think about my imaginary "dartboard." I am at the very middle of the dart-board. I have to make decisions, and all of the different people in my life are all around the bullseye. I have assumed that my family is going to be right there next to me, but that is not necessarily where they are. They are there and they are always going to be there, but often they are not the people who under-stand me best. And they don't have to understand everything I do. I can stop trying to justify myself all the time, expending energy, doubting myself, and worrying about not doing the right thing in their eyes.

People get so caught up in their families and feel that there is something wrong if they don't share everything with their family on a weekly basis. I think that is a huge expectation to have of anyone. They are your family, but you have different life trails. Keeping them in your life can be a great comfort and security, but they don't have to be your main support system. A lot of peo-ple think, "My mom doesn't really know me and I can't talk to my dad." I think that's normal. So many people grow up, never leave their home town, and never explore the world.

Learning how to talk to my family has been the trick. I can tell them, "You don't necessarily understand my situation and that's OK, but don't hound me for it." It's hard to do, but sometimes it's the most liberating thing in the world. Eventually, you create your own family, whether in the conventional sense or not. You develop a support network and a group of people that you feel com-fortable with. It will happen naturally. You will gravitate toward the people that you're supposed to be connected with, not the people that you are expected to be connected with. Let them be the ones who help you think about your work choices and life decisions.

deborah

Deborah, now 40, was the youngest person ordained an Itinerant Elder in the New Jersey Conference of the African Methodist Episcopal Church at age 24. After serving as Chaplain in the U.S. Navy for many years, she became the first African American woman to serve as a Dean of Religious Life and of the Chapel at Princeton University. Raised in both Mount Vernon, New York, and Newark, New Jersey, Deborah got her B.A. at Rutgers University, a Masters of Divinity at Interdenominational Theological Center, in Atlanta, Georgia, and a Masters of Theology at Princeton Theological Seminary in Princeton, New Jersey.

Princeton University is the playground for my godchildren, so I had to shift gears as I crossed campus for this interview. Usually I would stop to throw pebbles and climb on the statues with 2 and 3 year olds. This time I marched across campus and journeyed to the second floor of Murray-Dodge Hall and into Deborah's big, comfortable office. I knew she was older than many of the other women I interviewed but wanted her perspective included. She was one of the few women I talked with who had been the 'first' in her field.

As we talked across her coffee table she reminded me how many barriers have been broken by women like herself. Young women will walk much more easily into places like the Navy because of her work. She also reminded me how challenged people get by change and how much strategy is involved in creating change that will last. As I left, I was envious of the women at Princeton who had access to her as a role model on a regular basis. She challenged me to think about the role models in my life and the people who would be honest enough to tell me, "You might not want to go down that road."

DEBORAH'S STORY

I became a chaplain in the Navy and was stationed in Orlando, Florida. Historically, on Sundays there was an early church service that those of high liturgical interest attended. When my predecessor was leaving, my supervisory chaplain said, "When he leaves, you are going to be in charge." I thought, wow, what a great opportunity. So I revised the service a little bit. I didn't think that I did much, but in a short amount of time, the attendance went from 120 people to more than 800.

A colleague of mine viewed this old service with a new "twist" as somehow in competition with another service held earlier in the day. In a meeting he said he thought the service was more racial than religious. I knew what that meant, because I was the only African American woman on staff among all men of European decent. Consequently, another colleague and I met with our chaplain to work it out, and it was in that moment that I came to see that strategy was everything. My colleague helped me see that we needed to be diplomatic, but we also needed to make it clear that we didn't think it was a racial issue because everyone, people of many racial backgrounds, was coming to this service.

I learned through that situation that planning and setting up a strategy before the meeting helped to create a win-win situation for everyone. Eventually the chaplain saw that all types of people were in fact coming to the service, and that it wasn't about race, so he allowed it to continue.

When you are making a decision, too often there are not people around you who say, "You might not want to go down that road." It's not that they don't want to, but if you are successful and not really experiencing much chaos people often think you don't need voices of caution. But my colleague's perspective was important for me. I've since said to someone older, "I'm a lot younger than you and maybe you have been through something that I haven't. Your advice and counsel will be valuable to me."

What sometimes didn't work was trying to confront a system. Sometimes people are simply not willing to hear or change, even if they have the power to do so. I began to learn which battles to fight.

maria & rachel

The next two interviews happened simultaneously over a pan of lasagna in Richmond, Virginia. I had asked a friend to gather a few women from the area who were in the corporate world for a conversation about decisions during their 20's. Both of the women are married. Maria, 30, is a white woman who works in advertising. Rachel is a Chinese-Jamaican woman who works in sales.

Sitting with these women was a great wake up call for me. It reminded me how easily we slip into worlds where we interact with people of our own kind. I have spent most of my professional life in a non-profit world dominated by women and can't remember a time when I sat with a group of women to talk about the for-profit world. I was like a child in a candy store for the first time. Fascinated by their descriptions of their work worlds and the dynamics that they deal with on a regular basis.

They made me think about how much more we have to fight for on the road to equality for women and the ways we allow, or do not allow stereotypes to define and constrain us.

MARIA'S STORY

I've been in politics and I've been in advertising. In politics, the environment was dominated by men across the board. In advertising, even though I've worked with many women, the upper management and the key players are predominately men, by far. It is interesting that people have often said to me, meaning it as a compliment, "You're going to do well here because you are like one of the guys."

There is a stereotype in business that women are indecisive. Thus, I find myself at work in the mode that, if I make a decision, I'm going to stick with it if it kills me because of the stereotype that women are wishy-washy or flighty. The average age in advertising is about 30. It is such a young business, and you are dealing with a lot of young people who haven't really developed the poise or stature yet, so I think it is important to rise above and maintain that decisiveness all the time.

For me, the way to succeed is to be one of the guys. Even to the point that, if I'm on a business trip and I want nothing more than to go to bed but the guys are going to have a cigar or a drink at the bar, I'll suck it up and go to the bar with them. Usually when I'm traveling I'm the only woman, and you learn really quickly that all of the big decisions and discussions happen over dinner or drinks. You have to learn to go with it, to learn strategically where you need to go and when.

It is amazing to me how I respond to a male client versus a female client. I am more on guard with a male client and more aware of my actions, my responses, my poise – all to make sure he understands that I am capable and in control. It's as if I never want a male client to see my weak or soft side. It takes time to earn credibility, and I don't want to risk losing the respect and confidence I have gained.

In contrast, when working with a female client, it seems more acceptable to show a softer, more laid-back attitude. I find that I have gotten to know my female clients on a more personal level than my male clients. They are more willing to bring me into their lives and engage in personal conversations. It's as if women want to know about you and who you are in order to trust doing business with you, while men could not care less about your personal side just as long as you are qualified and up to the task at hand. Am I perpetuating a stereotype? I'm not sure, but I have observed this difference between male and female clients over and over again. And watching these trends has helped me do my job better.

RACHEL'S STORY

I've learned that being a woman in the workplace is very much like being a woman playing traditionally male sports. You are at a natural disadvantage because most of the rules have been set by the men, so you have to use your God-given assets and then adopt the other important skills you need in order to survive and make changes to this world. Success depends on making your colleagues, most of who are men, feel comfortable around you and, more importantly, respect you.

Growing up I was always really outgoing and felt lucky that I could get along well with people. I am not the "aggressive type," but I stand up for myself and am not afraid to voice my opinions. It is that easy balance of knowing when to listen and when to assert myself that has gotten me through in life and work. Also, I have been successful at work because I'm a team player.

I am now learning that as I climb the corporate ladder, I need to assert myself more often and not be afraid to take on conflict, even if it means not reaching a team consensus. This is difficult for many women like myself, since we have been taught to be harmonious, polite, and not to hurt others' feelings. Men on the other hand, are taught to exert their power and aggressiveness and to dominate the situation. As women climb the corporate ladder, learning to be assertive without hurting egos gets even tougher, since most of the players at that level are men, and the stakes are higher.

Many women have natural advantages, too. Rightly or wrongly, it helps your career when you are viewed as attractive, smart, and confident. I know I have been put in a situation to interface with some of our key customers because I am an attractive woman. Most of them are men, and when a buyer or customer is dealing with another man they are harsher and there is much more of a power play. When they are dealing with me, there is a softer tone. I am not as threatening to them. My boss uses me when he can and where he can. And I use my assets too. I'm successful at getting my way with people because I know my strengths as a woman.

Women also tend to be more intuitive than men. We tend to listen more closely and have a more innate sense of what is going on. This is an advantage over many men if used in the right way.

kim

Kim, age 36, grew up in Winston-Salem, North Carolina, and now lives in Asheville, NC. She majored in Spanish at Furman University and also has a Masters of Divinity from Southern Baptist Theological Seminary. She and her husband Stan pastored a church in Stoneville, NC, for several years before she returned to get her Masters of Fine Arts in Theatre for Young People at the University of Carolina at Greensboro. Kim loves performing and teaching mime. She currently juggles three part-time jobs that combine her love of young people and enjoyment of theatre. One of her proudest accomplishments was being Casey the Bat, the mascot for the Greensboro Bats minor league baseball team.

For several years I had worked with and loved Kim's husband. So it was a treat to sit in his office and listen to her talk about her life. His description of their partnership had inspired me for some time. Her aliveness as she told stories that wove together into a patchwork of her life's journey was magical to witness.

Her story reminded me of the power of our parents' choices on our own and the power of following our heart. She, like Deborah, walked a path traveled by very few women. She made me wonder about how men can be better allies to women in their journeys. I was glad to add her to my list of role models of women figuring out bold new partnerships with men.

KIM'S STORY

I grew up the daughter of a minister. My dad was good at it, and he loved it. I loved my dad, and I loved watching him do his job. It was pretty normal for me to want to follow in his path.

My sister once said, "My dad doesn't work, he just sits around and talks to people all day." I thought that was a pretty good job. I was lucky to be part of a church that encouraged me to explore many avenues as a youngster, and supported my decision to pursue ministry. I went to a student retreat before I went to Boston for my campus ministry internship. During the retreat, I felt that God was calling me to do something, to commit my life to ministry. I had not felt quite legitimate until I had this experience, because my Baptist tradition places a great deal of emphasis on the answer to the question, "When did you hear the call?"

When that feeling hit me, I felt like God's power was very big, very protective, very persuasive, and very wonderful. It was really comforting. It was as though a tide was carrying me forward toward the place where I was supposed to be.

There was definitely some resistance from others to my decision to go to seminary. At first I did not imagine being called to pastoral ministry because that was the most revered position – being the preacher of a church. It carries the most responsibility, power, and prestige. It also carries the most controversy because so few women do it. I downplayed the possibility of pastoral ministry because I was afraid people were going to tell me I couldn't do it, or that I would get the chance and I would fail. I tried to hang around the people who supported me and avoid those who didn't.

When I talked about my experience of being called, some people's comeback was, "You can't just go by your experience, you have to go by the Bible." At one point during seminary someone quoted scripture to me, saying that a woman can't hold authority over man and can't speak in the church. I said, "Aww, that's not in the Bible." I didn't know the Bible well enough to know that it *was* in there. I thought, God didn't mean that, that's ridiculous, but that argument didn't hold much weight with anybody who knew the Bible better than I did. However, I knew what felt right, and I paid attention to my instincts. I kept on the path toward ministry and ordination. It was hard, but I had to listen to what I felt was true inside. This was my place and what I needed to do.

I was 22 when I started seminary. During school I met Stan and got married. Stan and I decided we wanted to work together and he knew if we applied together, then I would have a better shot of finding a place to preach. At the time there were very few women serving as Baptist pastors. He helped open the door for me, so hats off to him.

We took a job co-pastoring in the small rural mill town of Stoneville, North Carolina. They had previously had two interim preachers, a husband and wife who did a lot of Bible study. They maintained that God calls everybody to ministry, and that in a church everybody has gifts. They encouraged the church to consider calling co-pastors on a longer-term basis. I remember one of the questions in our interview was, "What if the preachers don't agree." Our answer was "We'll vote in a business meeting like everybody else – we each get one vote." I think it was a little unnerving for the congregation to think there might not be one unified pastoral voice. We gave them a different picture of what ministry was like. It was a truly shared ministry.

We were 27 when we were hired, and we split one salary because we didn't need that much money. Since we were young, the church wanted us to help build the youth and children's program. We made friends and palled around with a lot of the young people. One day one of the teenagers called up. Stan answered the phone, and the kid said, "Yeah, is Kim there?" Stan said, "No." And the kid said, "Well, I guess maybe you can help. We're looking for some-one to play basketball; you want to play?" That was a sign that they were really responsive to me as a minister and as a regular person. To them it just wasn't any big deal that I was a woman. We were just Kim and Stan, their pastors. Which is the way it ought to be.

The women in the congregation would often introduce me proudly. Other times some members made jokes that they were in such rough shape they had to have *two* pastors. But I knew I was accepted when Stan went to visit an older couple in the congregation. When he drove up, their grandson, who was four and lived next door, saw the car go by. He ran after the car, screaming "Mom, the preacher is here, the preacher is here!" He ran to his grandpa and grandma's house and when he looked through the door Stan said, "Good morning." He turned around and went back home, looking completely dejected. When he got home he said, "Aww mom, that wasn't the preacher. It's that old man she's married to."

One of the hardest lessons of my job was to come to peace with different people's understandings of issues we faced. Our church was predominately white and we wanted to have a partnership with an African American church. We invited the other church to a fellowship meal and tried to start the ball rolling. Several members came to us and told us that a lot of people were resistant to it. A couple of people called up to tell us, "Other people don't want to hurt your feelings and tell you, but they don't like the idea of this partnership." It was as though we were dealing with phantom criticism because we couldn't address people who weren't coming to us directly. We tried to find a way to deal with this issue and be forthright about it. We also tried to honor the differences of opinion, because within the Baptist church that is one of the things we value – that everyone has the right to interpret the scriptures in the way they see fit, and in the way they can best understand it.

We were trying to balance how to stand firm for our convictions without forcing our convictions to be accepted. We found that a lot of people feared change, and we began to discover the power of being paid by the people that we preach to. Were we ready to leave the church over this? Were we ready to give up our income and our housing? What would we do?

In retrospect, I might have spent more time dealing with people's fear of changing and losing members. The church had just undergone a division before we came, and they didn't want to have that happen again. They were more committed to safeguarding their community than they were to going out on a limb. I learned that fear and prejudice can paralyze a church and keep it from taking a risk for God. Sometimes there is no way around it.

Afterwards, I blamed myself that it didn't turn out the way we thought it should. Sometimes, I find reasons to feel guilty about whatever happens, even when the responsibility is not mine. Part of my spiritual journey has been learning to affirm who I am and my gifts. When I trust God for acceptance, it helps me not be so desperate for other people's approval.

With kids, I don't feel desperate for their approval, but I get it hand over fist. I think it is partly because I am not trying to get their approval, and because I give mine to them. I found as church became more stifling and the demands of the institution became heavier, I retreated to the kids' class. I found that they were creative and honest and ready to embrace me. I remember one Christmas we were talking about what the angels did, and I asked, "So what's the main message of the angels?" And this little girl says, "Fear NOT!" I almost cried, because I was having such trouble facing my fears. I was having trouble with the church, with fear of being a failure, of not being able to fulfill the dream I had. The kids were able to articulate a depth of faith that was tremendous. They were able to include me as myself, and I have a magnetic pull toward them.

In the past I saw children's ministry as a secondary position in the church. I was so competitive that I really wanted to be the preacher and to prove I could do the big job. I put down the youth and children's ministry thinking, "People can do that in their sleep. It's no big deal, it's not as valuable." Now I'm finding I am much more at home with children and that's where I am choosing to be. Now I see it like this secret club — you can go in and do whatever you want, and as long as no adults come in, it's fine. There is permission there for me to be a kid, to see things with less baggage. It's a place where I find life and magic and enjoyment, because the kids remind me of what's most important.

choosing work

GUIDING QUESTIONS

- Which case study gave you new insight or made you think about some aspect of your life? How?
- What would it mean for you to follow your heart with a dream, a career, or a calling?
- When you think of finding meaningful work, what are your priorities? Money? People you will work with? Location? Freedom?
- What environment do you most enjoy? Do you like to work alone, with a team, with a supervisor? Do you want a mentor, or a group to manage?
- Who has influenced your major decisions in the past? Do you want them involved in your decision about work? Are there others you want to get advice from?
- If you are in a work situation currently, what is the hardest part of considering something new? Is it the search process, the changing of a routine, the relationships? What would you like to see change in your current situation?

ACTIVITIES

Write Your Work Autobiography

Imagine that it is 20 years from this date and you are reading your autobiography, which focuses on your work life. What have you done? Who are the people who noticed your talents? What is it about your work that gave you satisfaction? What is it that was difficult?

Map the Connections

On a sheet of paper, start by naming one person you know who might know something about the job you want. Who might that person know? Who else do you know? Getting the right job takes knowing the right people. Use whatever connections you can think of—your parents' friends, old teachers, employers, and friends. Map your way to people in the places you want to be.

Draw Your Dartboard

In Angie's story she speaks of the dartboard in her head, filled with the people who influence her decision-making process. What does your dartboard look like? Who is in the center, the bull's eye, of your decision-making process? Who is on the next tier, and the next? First map out the current state of your dartboard and then draw your ideal one. Who do you wish were influencing your decisions? Then compare your two dartboards. What would need to change for you to move from your current board to your ideal one?

Explore Your relationship With Work

Knowing what is important to you about work and your work environment is a key step in finding work that you love.
How do you respond to these questions?

    a. The most important thing about a job is that it pays a lot of money.

    b. The most important thing about a job is that I'm doing something I love.

    c. The most important thing about a job is whom you work with.

    d. The most important thing about a job is that you are making a difference in the world.

The Ideal Situation

In the ideal situation, I would get paid _____, have hours from _____ to _____, and my work would be located in _____.

The primary philosophy of the organization or company would include the following: (eg., commited to team building, focused on quality, working to help kids, etc.) _____ _____.

My future boss would be excited about me coming on board because of my _____ _____.

I also know that my ideal situation.... (is in a particular city, has certain benefits, etc.) _____.

Conduct an Informal Interview

Find a couple of people to talk to who do things you might want to do for work. Take it as seriously as you would an actual interview; you never know where it might lead. Some of the questions you might want to ask include:

- What is a typical day like in your position?
- What do you like about your job?
- What do you dislike about your job?
- What is important to you about this job?
- How did you get this job?
- How do you prepare for it?

Musts and Wants

Make a list of all the things that you feel you MUST have in a job situation (i.e., must be in New York City, must pay me at least $30,000, etc.). Then make a list of your WANTS (i.e., want to be a part of a team, want to have some say over the work environment, want to have a commute of less than 30 minutes). When you start your search you will have a better sense of what is important to you and what you are willing to let go of for the right opportunity.

sex, children
& abortion

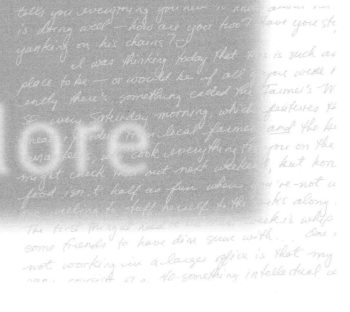

If there is a category of decisions that are more complicated and emotionally charged than the ones we make about children, I don't know it. So much of who we are, what we believe about life, God, and our feelings about others are tied up in decisions connected to sex, children, and abortion.

When I was younger, heavy weight rested on the question: Am I ready to have sex? Did I love my boyfriend enough? What would happen if I got pregnant? What would God think? What would my parents do if they ever found out? What would my friends say about me? Sorting through my thoughts and feelings on this topic at age 18 took almost a year. In the end, I ended up with the sexual policy that it was okay to have sex as long as I was positive that I was in love, and I was willing to raise a child with this man if for some reason birth control didn't work. As I've grown up, the decisions in this area of my life haven't been much easier. I am clearly in the post-sexual revolution generation.

Twenty-five years ago, women all over the country were breaking away from the expectations and rules about sex imposed on them by their religious institutions, parents, and schools. "MAKE LOVE NOT WAR" was proclaimed on college campuses, birth control became much more acceptable, and abortion was legalized. Greater space for pre-marital sex was created in bedrooms, dorm rooms, and back seats of cars.

Along with opened doors to sex before marriage, new openness has emerged for lesbian, bisexual and transgendered women. Young women feel more freedom in living and making choices about their sexuality and their lifestyles. Rather than being lesbian or being heterosexual, there are many women who identify themselves as bisexual. I have spent much more time than my mom thinking about my sexual identity, and I don't think I'm alone. While resistance to gay, lesbian, transgender and bi-sexual orientation is still very strong, there is a greater openness to talk about it and more support structures for women who identify as something other than heterosexual.

Another development, affecting the lives of all women in the past 20 years is the work that has been done to understand infertility. There are many new drugs on the market and millions of dollars being spent to assist the reproductive process for couples having difficulty conceiving. Many new books and guides have been published on the topic.

This is definitely an area of life in which options have exploded. Have kids or not have kids? If yes, through natural or artificial insemination? Is adoption an option? Whereas 20 years ago, a single 30 year-old woman might be assumed to be a lesbian, or strongly encouraged to join the convent, today I stand with scores of others and know that there are many acceptable options for me if I choose to become a parent.

Because women face so many decisions about sex, children and abortion, there are many related issues that arise. The case studies in this section capture just a few of them.

- Susan's story reveals the struggle involved in staying home with her child after having a successful corporate career. She talks about shifting relationships, accepting new sources of affirmation and having meaningful work.

- Susan continues her story with the details of dealing with infertility: the drugs, the doctors, and her emotions about all of it. There is little open dialogue about this topic for most of the general public, and she opens up a world that we are unlikely to know unless we are a part of it.

- Sarah talks about important connections between early sexual experiences and her present-day sex life.

- Maria and Rachel talk about anticipating the juggling act—trying to manage a professional career and have a life with children.

- Heather talks about her struggle to decide to have a child or to abort. She shares the process of getting into a grounded place and then making this major life decision.

- Gretchen describes finding herself pregnant shortly after getting married and the decision she made to have an abortion. She talks about bringing her husband along with her in the process and ending her own isolation.

susan

Susan is a wife and mother of one. She is a 31 year-old white woman who lives in Chapel Hill, North Carolina. After attending Wake Forest University and majoring in economics, she moved to Atlanta and then Dallas, Texas, where she met her husband.

I interviewed Susan twice about two different decisions she made in her 20's. The first was her decision to have a child. After spending the day at a mall with Susan and her daughter, we dropped her daughter home and went out on the town. Sitting in a crowded bar, eating dinner, Susan celebrated the space away from her daughter as she talked about the incredible experience of raising a child.

Her story made me think about the many women who are forced to make a decision between working and staying at home with their children. In addition to all of the logistics, the shift in her source of self-esteem from work to child-raising was a major challenge. As she spoke, she made me think about how much of my self-esteem comes from my work. I'm not sure what I would do if that source of affirmation disappeared.

SUSAN'S STORY

I was working at a consulting firm that helps companies figure out what benefits to offer employees. It was a big job for me. I was an integral part of a small company where I made good money and felt important. However, I didn't realize what I was gaining from that job until after I left to have my child and stay at home with her.

I used to think that as a mom I would have so much spare time. I imagined doing crafts and gardening, things I always wanted to do, but for which I never had time. Boy, was I wrong! I have a sister with kids and I should have known better, but I didn't. I used to say to stay-at-home moms, "It must be great, you must have so much time." They would laugh at me. Now I realize how demeaning that was.

Everyone tells you, "Get ready, your life is about to change. Get ready, your whole relationship with your husband is about to change. Get ready, everything that feels comfortable and secure is about to change." Yet despite all that advice, knowing my world was about to be rocked, there was nothing I could do to prepare to be a mom. Before my daughter Sarah was born, my husband Ted and I said we would be really good about having a date night every week and getting a babysitter. We didn't want our child to become the center of our universe. We wanted to continue to focus on our relationship because it is the most important foundation. We knew if we were not happy as a couple, our child would not be happy in our home. Then, the baby came along and all of these good intentions were thrown into the backseat.

The hardest thing has been to trust someone else with my child, to hand my baby over, even to my mother. I thought I would be comfortable trusting someone else for several hours, but I'm not. I'm getting better now that she is nine months old, but that was the first difficulty that I thought we would handle well. It was a joke.

Having a baby takes you by storm. You go home from the hospital with no idea of what you're doing. Then, all of a sudden, you are the expert on your own child. It is not like today you are going to spend an hour being a mommy and start getting used to it, and then tomorrow you will spend five hours. It is not a gradual process. You start at the hardest place. I remember delivering Sarah and being so exhausted and thinking, "Oh, now I can rest." Hello – I don't think so! You nurse her through the night for three days at the hospital, sleep deprivation sets in immediately, and it doesn't end. You think, I can take three days of this and then I will catch up, or two weeks and then I will catch up. But you don't. For me, who always needed ten hours of sleep a night, it slammed me hard. With no transition time, you step immediately into a state of total sleep deprivation. While in this state it is your responsibility to care for an absolutely needy infant. At times they cry for no reason and you can't solve the problem. You start there in the hardest place, and thank God, it gets easier.

At two months the baby sleeps through the night, if you are lucky. You then wake up to notice you've neglected your husband for two months. So the whole relationship with your husband that you worked so hard on goes downhill from day one. Both of you are totally in love and share a wonderful child, but you neglected each other for at least two months and you are so sleep deprived that if he drops a towel on the floor you are ready to murder him. Both of you are at your wit's end. Three months into it you've been so focused on your child that you turn around and ask, "What's happened to our relationship? Why are we so mean to each other? Why don't we even want to be around each other?" It takes another six weeks to figure out what is going on in each other's heads.

I was adjusting to a million different factors that I couldn't explain or identify. To complicate matters, I chose to quit work and stay home. Adding to that, we moved across the country to a new city when Sarah was three months old. It took me another three months to see that this change was rocking my world. Before Sarah's birth it would have taken me three days to figure out what was bothering me, not three months. I finally realized that I went from people telling me every day at work, "You are doing an incredible job," and clients saying, "I don't know what we would do without you," to keeping company with a wailing infant. A great deal of my self-esteem had come from my job. Now I had to find self-esteem some other way and I didn't know where to start.

As a stay-at-home mom you get very little respect. If I think about getting into a conversation, I know the first question anybody will ask is, "Oh, what do you do?" They don't ask what religion you are or what sign you are. They ask you what you do for a living. When you say you are a stay-at-home mom the conversation ends there.

After three months I realized I got no validation at home, and that I was having an identity and power crisis. Ted would work with me on the validation issue by coming home and saying, "You're such a great mom." I felt it was such a worthless compliment. It felt patronizing. How did he know? I would say, "Don't tell me I'm a great mom because you don't know." How do you measure anyway? Well, I changed ten dirty diapers today and I really wiped that butt clean. That sounds terrible, but it's real. We realized that Ted couldn't be the only person to validate me, that I needed to seek support in other places. If I waited for my child to offer it, it could take thirty years. My validation now comes from talking with other women who are going through the same thing, or have been through it. I call my sister and say, "I know I am going insane – I am depressed, I'm feeling like a worthless mother, I'm sure my daughter would be better off without me." And my sister will say, "That is so normal. You are feeling what every first-time mother feels and this is why." She will list at least ten reasons why I feel this way. Having shared experiences with other women is enormously important in getting through the first year of isolation and change with your new child.

I knew I needed a new support system, so I joined a group of stay-at-home moms, who used to work outside the home. At meetings I hear what many other women are going through. The support group is part of a network that meets twice a month all over the country. It provides an opportunity for women who stay at home or work part-time to go somewhere without their children, to discuss things with other adults, and have a social component as well.

Having your first child brings amazing changes for which you cannot be prepared. My advice to someone about to become a new parent is to promise yourself to let go of all the pretenses of life. . . don't worry if you're in your PJ's at noon, or if the house is a disaster for three months. Just let it go and try to grow through all the changes. Let them happen and, in the end, the good Lord makes you forget the bad parts and remember the good.

susan, con't

After we talked the first time, I returned to Susan's home several months later. Her large house was half decorated. She had just finished painting the living room days before. Her husband had put her daughter to bed and we sat on her soft, large couch as I probed a bit more into her life and her decision-making process. This time she spoke of her difficulties in conceiving her daughter.

Once again I found myself in a foreign world, fascinated by the details. Our conversation made me wonder what was going on with the rampant infertility problems she described. I was curious why I hadn't heard more about an issue that is affecting so many women.

SUSAN'S STORY, CON'T

Most women in their twenties don't know that there are a lot of people having trouble getting pregnant. All you see are examples of people who have children and people who don't. You don't notice and you don't ask questions. Many couples are having trouble. For many people, not being able to conceive is a painful secret. I could name 15 friends who are dealing with infertility in varying degrees, so it must be very prevalent. It is unfortunate that there is not more information getting to young women.

My husband and I always wanted children. We wanted a child about a year before it actually happened. In our immediate-gratification world, you go along, advancing your career, and talk about having children at some point off in the future. Then suddenly you decide to have a child. When it doesn't happen in three or six months, you start worrying about it. The worrying only makes it worse and even less likely that you will conceive because a tremendous amount of pressure builds.

Doctors used to say, "Go try for a year, don't worry about it." People would wait a couple of years before they would even seek treatment. Treatment is much more prevalent now because doctors are much more willing to jumpstart the process. I don't know if that is good or bad, but it is the reality.

We were lucky because my doctor said, "Whenever you want to start having children, you need to come talk to me." He knew I was going to have problems because my system is irregular. We began with a full hormone check on my husband and me.

Through the whole infertility process, one of the things I found most disturbing was how many physicians were doing something other than the recommended treatment. There is lots of bad advice out there, and trusting your doctor blindly is not always the best strategy. I was lucky enough to find a great book, *The Infertility Sourcebook*. It describes the steps a doctor should lead you through and has details about many conditions. I've handed out a half a dozen copies to friends.

The process is often long and frustrating. First, they do a blood and semen check to rule out several possible problems. My problem was that I had lots of eggs, but they did not release. They put me on a drug that tells the brain to produce a missing hormone. After three months we knew that drug didn't work.

Then I did another test in which they cleaned out my fallopian tubes to make sure there isn't any blockage, a procedure that sometimes resolves a woman's infertility problems. There are lots of unpleasant procedures through the whole process which make it even more difficult to handle emotionally. On top of that you have a lot of insensitive doctors who deal with infertility every day. They treat you like you are in for a broken arm, while you are just dying inside because you're thinking you won't ever have a child. A failed month is really tough. It is an emotionally devastating process.

After several months we went on to the next step, taking an injectable hormone that produces eggs. Every night for ten days, my husband Ted had to give me a shot in my thigh. During this period, I visited the doctor's office every few days for sonograms and blood work. On the fourteenth day of my cycle I went into the doctor's office and had artificial insemination. This procedure places the sperm in an optimum spot in your uterus for conception and increases your chances of conceiving. Ted went in the morning to produce the sperm sample and then he said, "I'll see you later." I said, "No way, you are coming to the doctor's office with me." So he was there for the conception. Although it was very unromantic, we did conceive. Sarah was born nine months later.

During this difficult process I got involved in an infertility support group. I met incredibly strong women, and I looked at them and said to myself, there is nothing wrong with me. It interrupted a lot of my self-pitying moments. Some of the women had six and seven miscarriages, sometimes at 3 or 3 1/2 months when they thought they were safe—and they were so strong speaking about it.

From the time we started, it took us a year to conceive. We have a fortunate story. There were women in my support group who had been trying for years, and what they went through every single month was incredible. It is amazing what a couple will do to conceive. It seemed to me that the longer the infertility went on, the more it became a mission for these women, that they were going to do anything to get pregnant. At the same time I watched the husbands become more and more unsupportive or want to give up. It was really sad. I think the men pulled back emotionally and gave up way before the women did.

I was so blessed to have a husband who said, "All right, where do I give my sample?" It was no big deal to him at all. Some men would say, "I'm not doing that!" Many women were getting their bodies poked and prodded and violated in horrible ways by their doctors in order to conceive and to have their husbands be resistant was devastating. Infertility can definitely divide and conquer a couple. We were lucky that it brought us closer together.

On top of the emotional pressure for both men and women, there is tremendous financial pressure. If a health plan covers infertility at all, it usually covers only 50 percent of the bills. Typically you have to pay for your medications completely, which can be anywhere from $500 to $1200 a month. The infertility process cost us about $5,000, and that was with 90 percent of our medical costs covered.

Ted and I both agree now that we are glad we went through the process. Sarah is such a blessing, and the struggle to conceive made us appreciate our little gift even more. Even though we struggled enormously, the process brought us together and made us stronger.

sarah

Sarah, 31, is an Irish Catholic woman who lives in Brooklyn, New York. After graduating from Connecticut College and majoring in Political Science, she moved to New York to work in the publishing industry. Eventually she began to tutor and then teach in the New York City Public Schools.

I knew Sarah from my days as a youth worker, but hadn't seen her in several years when I bumped into her in New York. We ended up sharing a bus ride between New York and Boston. As the bus rolled north, we began talking about what we were doing with our lives and one thing led to another. As I described the book, she was fascinated. I asked her if she was interested in me interviewing her. She said yes, but we never got to the interview. She agreed instead to write about one of the most significant choices she made during her 20's. Here it is.

As I read her story of facing fear she made me think of the many other women along my journey whom I had talked to about dealing with sexual abuse as a major factor in their development during their 20's. It made me wonder how many women are impacted by sexual abuse who don't talk about it and what we are doing as a culture to make this topic so taboo. Her story challenged me to think about what fears I run from, and how I might feel if I walked head-on into them.

SARAH'S STORY

I remember the exact moment that the blurry sketch of the memory hit me. I was walking down H Street in D.C. on my way home after work. It was cool for the spring and the night was pitch black. I had just passed the house on the corner that I dreaded passing every night. Kids were always outside, screaming and hitting each other. A small gang of adults usually hung out at the bottom of the steps and on the sidewalk, smoking and playing loud rap music. My whole body tensed up as I walked by, keeping up my front of composure until I got far enough away to breathe again.

I was three houses down the street when a picture showed up on my mental screen. I saw my bed, pushed up against the wall and covered with a white eyelet comforter. My cousin was pushing up against me, I was struggling to push him off.

I stopped right in the middle of the street. I leaned back against the stone wall along the sidewalk. I said to myself, what was this picture about? Was it real? Was I making it up? Why am I remembering this right now? No, it couldn't have been real, could it?

After a few minutes of stillness, I mechanically walked home and went up to my room. I ignored the memory as much as I could for a few days. Each time it reentered my mind there was a new detail. I started writing about it in my journal, forcing myself to figure out whether it was real or a figment of my imagination. A month later I was talking to a friend, and I told him I was really scared that maybe I had been sexually abused when I was young, but I was really confused about it. Maybe I had liked it? Maybe I was a part of it? Maybe it was true? It didn't phase him. He told me that when he was young his cousin forced him to suck his penis. He said it with no charge, no shame, and no embarrassment. He said it as if he had said, "Yeah, I used to go visit that zoo, too." He asked me, "What is the worst thing that would happen if it was true?"

I looked out the window of the car and thought for a few minutes. Then I said, "Everyone would think I was a slut and that I had sex with my cousin, the worst sin possible." As I said it a piece of the cinder block resting on my shoulder crumbled away. There it was. The worst possible scenario. I knew I wasn't the only one who had explored their body with their family, and I wasn't the first woman to feel violated by a family member. At that point I figured that there was no other solution than to begin making peace with the possibilities of my past.

That was one of the most significant decisions I made in my twenties. Instead of continuing to run from the possibility of sexual abuse and incest, I was going to face it.

As a result of this early sexual experience, I had lived years of my childhood terrified and never told anyone. I walked downstairs that night and sat at the dinner table, ready to burst out of my skin and explode onto the kitchen table. Instead, I kept it in, giving no clues to anyone. I was excused as soon as possible, went back up to my room, hugged my bear, and fell asleep. For the next ten years the secret stayed locked in my subconscious.

As a good Catholic girl, I understood that pre-marital sex and incest were two of the worst sins. I contemplated suicide regularly, should my secret be leaked. I didn't dare tell anyone what had happened. It is still unclear to me when I lost the memory of it. During my teens and twenties I ran from activity to activity, praying no one would notice my terror and shame. As my memories emerged, I remembered that I spent at least a year after the incident convinced I was pregnant. I hadn't yet gotten my period, and I didn't know enough about pregnancy to know better. As I waited for my period to come, I grew more and more sure that I was going to have to deal with the horrible possibilities growing in my mind.

A few years after the incident I had a grand mal seizure in church, which makes sense to me now. Completely unconscious, back arched over the pew, shaking all over, my secret was struggling to get out of me in some way.

I had another seizure when I was 22, a month after I first recalled the memory. For the second time in my life I waited for doctors and MRI machines to confirm that there was nothing wrong with me. I hadn't yet told anybody about the memory. I spent two weeks unable to move off my couch. During that time I realized that I had to change the way I was living. I had to stop running from my fears and my emotions.

I stopped pumping myself full of caffeine and quit an 80-hour-a-week job. I cried for the first time that I could remember since my high school graduation. I got involved in a co-counseling class, where my peers learned how to counsel me and I them. I began letting go of the illusion that I was always "Great!" and began reconnecting to my body after years of terror-induced distance. I got involved with a man who was emotionally available and who helped me come to peace with my body and my fears about sex and intimacy.

I let him hold me while I cried out the years of fear. I even began to figure out how to talk to my family about my memories. I tried over and over again to slow down my life enough so I could feel something.

I will say that facing that my memories has been one of the most powerful decisions in my life and the one with the most challenging consequences. I've been forced to look at how hard it is for me to think about sex, men and getting close to people. I see how scared I am of saying what I really feel and of having my physical boundaries violated. I've watched myself put walls up with my best friends because I have been scared that they too would violate my body, even when that was the most unlikely thing in the world.

With information I've gotten from my cousin's sibling, I know that some weird things around sex happened when we were young. I haven't yet had a direct conversation with my cousin involved in the memory. I've been waiting to feel ready to accept his denial if it is there. I know that this is common. A victim confronts an abuser and they deny it completely. I want to feel stronger before I move on to that. I have talked to others in my family and already I've run into their denial: "That couldn't have happened. You must be connecting this to some other memory." They are probably as scared as I was to face the possible truth. I'm still not sure I know the complete story, but I do know that I was too terrified to talk about whatever happened and that it's had a major impact on me.

One of the hardest feelings is that I lost an important battle back then. I wasn't physically strong enough to protect myself and I wasn't brave enough to speak up about what happened. Instead I became hopeless and silent. Writing has played a major role in reclaiming my voice. I've been able to tell the truth – at first to myself, and gradually to others. I remember the first night I wrote out my memory; I felt like a woman walking out of a jail cell. The terror and shame were loosening their hold on me.

I have had intense counseling sessions about the memory, and my life has changed dramatically. I can now feel my body instead of being numb most of the time. I can now feel comfortable voicing my boundaries and expecting friends and sexual partners to respect them.

I still have struggles in this area. I think it is something I will deal with for the rest of my life. But I also feel that making the decision to face my greatest fear has led to many other courageous decisions. It's like a domino effect. You make one bold decision, and then you make another, and another. Before you know it, instead of being a trapped, quiet, scared woman you feel like a bold, powerful, creative giant. Now it isn't so hard for me to say, "Yeah, this is the worst possible scenario if my fear becomes real," and then walk right into it.

maria & rachel

This is a continuation of the conversation in the Work chapter of
two married women involved in the corporate world. They continued to teach me about their home and work lives. Their con-
cerns about childrearing and promotions weren't familiar to me.
Although I know many women struggle with the balance between
work and family life, it is one I have not faced. It made me question the expectations we continue to put on women to do it all.
It made me wonder what I would do if I did have to make a
choice between my work and raising a family.

MARIA'S STORY

One aspect of my advertising work is that I have clients all over the country.
My job is account management, so the task of building the client relationship
depends primarily on me. I have to be out on the road as much as possible,
bringing concepts and strategies to clients. I was home for only three months
last year. Now that I am 31 and starting to think about a family, I am struggling with the thoughts of balancing such an insane work schedule and a baby.
I can't imagine it. Even when I am not traveling, my work often hits full force
at the end of the day. When I think I will be home by 5:30 p.m., I get a call at
4:30 p.m. that means I need to stay until 9:00 p.m.

Until now, I have been 100 percent work focused and very driven in my
career. But now that some of my friends have children, being the company's
number-one performer suddenly doesn't seem like such a priority. As I am
getting older my priorities are changing, and spouse and family need to
come first.

Advertising is such a young business. I think this is because a lot of women
get into their thirties and leave. They can't balance the crazy hours and family.
When ads need to get out the door and clients call needing a change for the
next day, you don't leave. Day care closes at 5:30 p.m. If you are trying to pick
up kids, you're stuck. When your work is serving clients, there is no working at

home, no telecommuting. It's a collaborative business; the bosses want people to work together, to bounce ideas off of one another.

Most women I know get out of the business entirely when they have children. I know a few who have babies and are still working. They are really struggling and putting a lot of stress on their spouses. Some have chosen to be the "provider" and their husbands stay at home to watch and nurture the kids. Everyone has their own choices to make, but having my husband stay home while I work is not an option for me—I would feel that I am somehow missing out on my child's growth and development.

I'm thinking that I have two years to figure out what I am going to do next. The women who have tried to stay in advertising and raise kids are super-women, but they are also willing to leave their kids for a month. I don't think I can do that. It makes me sad to think that I can't do both, but if I do, I know I will do neither well.

RACHEL'S STORY

The majority of my job involves face-to-face interaction with our customers and sales representatives. This means that I am on the road 30-40 percent of the week, keeping my finger on the pulse of the marketplace. This is what I am good at, and also what my company considers essential to becoming a senior manager in the division. The marketplace changes so quickly, and we learn by being out there on the front line.

When I decide to start having a family, it will affect my career. In the short term, I will have to cut back on travelling which will diminish my experience in the marketplace and reduce my chances at becoming senior manager of my division. The alternative is to leave the baby at home three days a week with a nanny, which I am not sure I emotionally can or want to do. My husband is willing to help, but he is a lawyer and is also competing with other men at work, many of whom have wives who stay at home to take care of all the household tasks. The ultimate responsibility of taking care of the baby will likely fall on me. The choice of having a family and a career means that I will have to "give" on something.

As a potential solution, I am trying to work with my boss to forge a more strategic support position within the division that doesn't require as much travelling. But the fact is, although he hasn't said it, he sees it as a step back; I am in essence making a choice.

heather

Heather, 26, lives in Seattle with her daughter Asha. She grew up in rural upstate New York and attended Seattle University where she majored in sociology. After school she stayed in the city and became the director of youth programs in a non-profit. Currently, she is teaching 2nd and 3rd grade in the Seattle Public Schools.

I met Heather a year before our interview while I was out in Seattle for work. Many people recommended we talk. When we met over oatmeal in a funky Seattle cafe, she told me she just found out she was pregnant. I knew we would cross paths again. So I was not surprised to find myself a year later in front of her with her 6 month-old daughter at our feet.

Heather found herself pregnant at a time when she hadn't planned it. Heather was one of the few women I met who seriously considered an abortion and decided to have the child. As I talked with her I knew that I could have easily been in her shoes. She made me wonder what I would do if I found myself pregnant. Her decision made me ponder the abortion question more deeply.

HEATHER'S STORY

Most of my life, all I wanted to do was travel. I had saved up about $4,000 to go to India, Asia, and Vietnam when I found myself pregnant.

I knew that I was probably going to get pregnant. I had unprotected sex, so I went to Planned Parenthood and got the morning-after pill. I felt awful for a few days but thought everything was cool. I went along, waiting and waiting to get my period. One day I got so nauseous I couldn't get to work until 11:00. Finally I decided I should probably take a pregnancy test.

It really didn't hit me right away; I was dumbfounded. I called the guy I was seeing at the time, thinking to myself, "I'm pregnant with a guy who is 47, 20 years older than me. He even has kids older than me. He's a former Black Panther from a really different walk of life. On top of it, he's legally married. Oh my God."

I lived for weeks tossing the decision back and forth in my mind. Was I going to have an abortion or was I going to have a baby? I was in transition, sleeping on a friend's couch. I struggled to get myself centered enough to make a good decision.

I saw a counselor a couple of times, and she had me write a list of pros and cons. She had me envision myself having a baby and then envision having an abortion. When I tried to imagine having an abortion, I couldn't even get in the car. That's how strong my feelings against having an abortion were. Deep down inside I knew that I couldn't do it; it just took me a while to get to a clear place. I'm glad that I waited to make my decision, that I took the time I needed to get grounded. If I hadn't, I might have gone to my Planned Parenthood appointment.

I pushed the date back again and again until it was the last day the abortion could be scheduled. Before I called the clinic I called my mom and said, "Mom, I'm pregnant." She said, "I'll support you with whatever you do." I needed to have the affirmation from her. Then I called the clinic and canceled my appointment. At 25, I decided I was going to have a baby.

My father passed away from a long bout with cancer when I was 15. I learned a lot from that experience, which gave me a strong sense of strength. I knew I could raise this child. I figured, I have a degree, I have been to a lot of places in the world, I love myself, I have confidence, and I can do it.

I learned that when you make a decision this big, you need to be in a centered place. I knew what to do, but there was so much else going on in my head. I surrounded myself with people who supported me, no matter what decision I made.

Asha, my daughter, is such an important part of my life. I can't imagine her not in this world. It's exciting and scary, and I would be lying if I said there weren't some days that I didn't wonder what my life would be like if I had followed through with the abortion. I have a feeling I wouldn't be as happy.

gretchen

Gretchen, who is also represented in the Work chapter, made one decision about work and following her dreams and another one about her family. With a new marriage and emerging career as an entrepreneur she decided to have an abortion. She was an exception to most of the women I talked to who had abortions. She talked about her experience easily, openly and without any excuse. It was a refreshing glance at what is possible for other women who still hold a lot of guilt and shame about their decisions.

Her story brought up the importance of bringing men along with us in our decisions about our bodies. She didn't just invite her husband to join in the process, she demanded it. She showed how a painful experience can open us and strengthen our relationships. Her story showed me the important role of men in supporting us to become stronger women.

GRETCHEN'S STORY

I was going along, living my life, knowing I wasn't ready to have a family, and luckily never having to make a decision about it even though I had had an active sex life since I was about 16. Surprise, surprise, right when we got married, I got pregnant. It might have been on our wedding night. Making the decision not to start a family at that time was really clear.

As women, especially Catholic women, we are taught to be "young ladies" without lust or sex. Then you begin to lust, to have sex, and how are you supposed to deal with it? We have so many uncomfortable sexual situations and no one talks about them, and you think you are at fault. The guilt starts piling up. When I needed to talk to my mom I couldn't, and once I could talk to her, I didn't need to anymore.

When I became pregnant, I said to my husband, "You need to talk with me about this and we will both go through this together." It could have been a painful experience but instead it was empowering. With my husband's support, I felt that I could make a decision about my body and be supported in it. Since then I've had times when I have battled with the clock, feeling I have to hurry up and have children. The hardest time was in my late twenties when I was thinking seriously about children. But I had too much going on. I figured if you just let it go by, it's not that big a deal. Your life is long and you have plenty of time to decide if you want to have a family, if you want to do that.

I wonder what comes first when making a decision: the cart or the horse. I'm 31 now and I'm really glad I went through my twenties without kids. I went to college. I quit. Then I went back. I started an Internet cafe with my husband and other friends, and I've been able to educate myself much more than I thought I would. I couldn't have done a lot of these things if I had had kids right away. I keep getting younger the older I get because I get more in touch with how I was when I was young. I think all of these things will help me be a better mom, when and if we decide to have kids.

sex, children & abortions

- Which case study gave you new insight or made you think about some aspect of your life? How?
- If you don't have children, what do you think about having children? What do you imagine will be the biggest trade-off in having kids?
- What should we be teaching young women about sex, birth control, and abortions that you might not have known growing up?
- If you've had an abortion, how do you feel about it? If you could have more support in processing your feelings around your decision, what form would it take?
- If you do have children, what would it look like to be completely supported? How might you get more support in your life?

EXERCISES

if you don't have children

Create Sexual Principles

Many women end up pregnant when they are not ready. Could you be one of them? Think hard about protection if you are having sex, and don't rely strictly on a condom. Talk with friends about where it gets hard for you to think in the area of sex. Make a list of ways you stop thinking or are silent around sex. What would help you have a greater ability to think in this area? Consider creating some sexual principles for yourself that guide your sexual life such as:

- no sex when you're drinking or under the influence of drugs
- no sex before marriage
- sex only with protection
- sex only when there is a strong emotional connection

Interview a Mom

If you are not a mom, find one and ask her some questions about having children. Questions might include:

- What is the best thing about being a mom?
- What is the hardest thing about being a mom?
- What is the most surprising thing about being a mom?
- If you could play rewind on getting pregnant, giving birth, and raising your child, are there things you might do differently? What are they?

Get Children in Your Life

If you want children in your life and don't have them, make it a priority. There are children everywhere who are in need of love and attention. Find a friend or relative with children and build a relationship with them. Take them to the zoo, stop by to read a story before bed, or take them to the library.

if you have children

Explore a Support Group for Moms

There are a variety of support groups for moms. They range from groups like the La Leche League, which helps women who are breastfeeding, to FEMALE, a group that supports women making the transition from corporate America to child care. Talk to moms in your area or look in a community phone book for local resources for mothers.

Start a Co-Op or Play Group

One way to get more support in your life is to spend time with other mothers who are also trying to balance the work of childrearing. Co-ops can offer you free babysitting in return for babysitting you do for other people's children, and play groups can be a helpful way to break the isolation parenting can bring.

Invite Friends Without Children to Play a Role in Your Children's Lives

There are many people who don't have children of their own, but would love to have children as part of their life. Invite friends to take adventures with your kids, to stop by to read stories at night after work, or to make a weekly date. It might help you expand your support base.

depression, addiction & abuse

explore

There are many decisions regarding depression, addiction and abuse that don't seem quite like decisions. We don't choose to get depressed, be addicted to a substance or be abused. But we do have a choice in how we respond to these challenges. How will you deal with depression if you find yourself in one? Who or what will you turn to if you are wrestling with a drug, alcohol, or food addiction? And if you have a history of sexual or domestic abuse, will you respond by running or getting support to heal?

During my 20's, depression, addiction and abuse entered my life in a variety of ways. At the time, I had no idea how common my situation was. As I listened to women talk, I realized I was not alone. One was struggling with a drug addiction, another working with a therapist to process intense childhood sexual abuse, still another talked about depression and her decision not to take the drugs a doctor encouraged her to take. As I listened I began piecing together a new picture. I was getting the sense that most of us had some demon hiding in our closet that we hoped others would not discover. They were what most of us consider the "ugly", "weak," and "undesirable" part of our past and present.

What I see now, however, is that a tremendous amount of energy is expended to keep these secrets hidden. In response to what I was discovering, I found myself sharing more and more of my struggles with women who I met and interviewed. Their stories were extra encouragement to let go of the image of having it all together. A small chain reaction began. As I revealed more of my struggles to new women I met, they became more comfortable sharing their challenges with me.

When I began these conversations I did not know the facts. Later I researched and discovered:

- The highest risk population for depression today is late adolescents and young adults. More than one-third of women in the age range of 18-22 are showing significant depression. (Sheehy, *New Passages*, 47)
- 4.5 million women in this country have a drinking problem. And 43 percent of Alcoholics Anonymous members are women under the age of 30. (Trebilcock, 66)
- 17.7 million, or 17.6 percent of women in the U.S. have been the victim of an attempted or completed rape. (RAINN Facts)

In deciding how to deal with depression, addiction, or abuse, women find all types of support and assistance. Some choose doctors, therapists, psychologists, or prescription drugs. Others choose support groups, meditation or writing. Everyone has their own healing process. The unfortunate side of the story is that too many people stay silent. In Richard O'Connor's book, *Undoing Depression: What Therapy Doesn't Teach You and Medication Can't Give You,* he talks about this happening with people who are depressed:

> Many people who have had severe depressions report that they suffered for years, sometimes decades, before they told anyone. They felt so isolated and so self-blaming that they assumed there was nothing to be done, nothing that anyone would understand. Meanwhile they "passed" —they went right ahead with life, putting on a happy face and achieving success in schools, in careers, in the family. (73)

The women in this chapter are those who have chosen an alternate route, and have decided to be honest with themselves and the people around them about their struggles. Each woman found her own process and made unique choices about how she would respond.

- In her description, Firkins talked about what she gained from her depression. "Life got round" and ceased to feel strictly linear. She found that depression brought her closer to God.

- Are we allowed to fully retreat through depression? Chris asks as she tells her story of depression after the birth of her second child. She explores the possibility that depression allowed her to become integrated.

- Yu-lin found meditation as a powerful way to move on from a challenging childhood. She learned how to listen to herself, "rather than the babble of insecurities."

- When Laura was taken by surprise by panic attacks in her mid-twenties she didn't know where to turn for help. She explains her process of searching for support and learning the connections between her anxiety and her brother's depression.

- Sharia chose strength when she had the option to face or hide from her history of sexual abuse. She talks about the role of silence in perpetuating abuse and the power in developing the ability "to turn anger and negative energy into something productive."

- As she dove into the challenge of facing her alcohol addiction during her twenties, Cara's struggle was to realize her connection with others. She describes a powerful relationship with her brother, who was also dealing with addiction.

- Jenny talks about her addiction to Nutrasweet and food and what it took for her to change the way she thought about and treated her body.

- Figuring out how to support a friend who is dealing with depression was Edith's challenge. She offers insight into how the experience strengthened her relationship with her friend.

firkins

Firkins, 38, grew up in northern Vermont and has spent most of her life in New England around educational institutions. After getting her B.A. degree from Harvard-Radcliffe while serving as co-captain of the ice hockey team, she earned a Masters in English from Middlebury's Bread Loaf School of English. A few years later she got her Masters from Harvard's Graduate School of Education. She has spent many years teaching English to both high school and college students. A lover of adventure, she spent two summers in Kenya doing volunteer development work and, during a nine-month solo-journey through Asia, worked in refugee camps in Thailand. Currently she lives in Cambridge, Massachusetts, with her husband and their two small children Zoey and Mia.

She was one of my early role models in this process. The first woman I interviewed. As we sat at her home in Cambridge, sipping tea and talking about her life she spoke with all of the confidence I wanted. She talked about the miraculous way things seemed to fall into place once she let go of trying to control her life and her depression. At the time I knew it was what I wanted to learn how to do.

Although she is a teacher, she might as well have been my therapist. I returned to her kitchen table several times during the 2 1/2 years it took to create this book. Each time she left with me with some simple, yet timely piece of wisdom that I needed at the moment. Her story reminded me that you have to let go if you want the rewards to follow.

FIRKINS' STORY

It was a hard year. Torn from my routine as a teacher and living suddenly in a house full of strangers, I fell into a deep depression.

In the beginning I was afraid that if I let myself fall apart, I would never get back together again. I asked my therapist about this, and I remember her reply, "There are never any guarantees, Firkins." For some reason, this answer was helpful. Far from being scary, it actually freed me. It was an answer of truth, capturing the ambiguity right at the center of things. At a certain point, however, I had no choice but to fall apart. I could no longer pretend to be functioning normally, to be feeling anything other than fragile and sad. I spent many days in bed, crying and sleeping, just staring at the ceiling above my bed. But I didn't blow apart completely, and the world didn't end. I realized I could let things go, even fail, and still be okay.

I see now that in many ways I'd been running from myself for many years. I'd been aware at different times of this other self, a sadder self – what had always felt like a truer self – nipping at my heels. I'd always been too afraid to confront it, too terrified the darkness would consume me if I turned to face it. But, finally, I just couldn't go on anymore. I was tired, worn out from running, and unable to keep finding patches of light. I was unable to continue being divided from myself. Until I owned all parts of me, I could not find meaning in my life. I remember my therapist asking me early on how long I had felt this way – two weeks, two months? Clearly she was worried about me. I looked at her and smiled a weak smile. "How about fifteen years," I replied. "Now that I think about it, I can't remember ever not feeling this way."

It was in my depression that life got round. It ceased to feel strictly linear. Life began to feel more spiritual, like the motion of a spiral. I'd always had a line to follow, goals to accomplish. This is what I'd been taught. College, graduate school, jobs, looking ahead to love and marriage – but suddenly, even though I was in graduate school at the time, none of that mattered. Once I realized I wasn't going to dissolve, my concern shifted. I only wanted to stay in this sad space long enough. I knew I was healing and that it would only happen in this place of sorrow. In a more profound way than I had when traveling, I was confronting my most terrifying fears. I was "unwriting" false stories I'd created about myself.

One day from this time stands out. It was a chilly morning in January. I'd awakened early, overwhelmed, afraid, floundering in my despair. I'd spent the day before in bed, sobbing, immobile, frozen in sadness. This particular morning, I found myself in my car, in my pajamas and parka, not sure where I was headed. "Look at me," I remember saying out loud. "Look at me. I'm a mess." I was sobbing, "I'm lost. I'm so damn lost."

I ended up at Michael and Jen's, my former roommates. At the time, Michael was in social work school. Jen had just finished divinity school and was studying for the deaconate. I was sitting on their stoop in a heap when Michael opened the door. Obviously I'd woken them up. His hair went in every direction and he still had on his pajamas. I couldn't even say hello. I just started crying. They pulled me into their bed. They held me while I sobbed. "Why?" I kept asking. "Why? Why all this pain and sadness? Why all this dark?"

I was sobbing, choking on my tears, but Jen just looked at me and smiled. "I'll tell you why," she said. "There's a reason. Let me tell you a story." Then she told me about a priest, one she knew from her hometown. He'd suffered two years of depression, two years of searing pain, she said, and his demand to know why went many years without an answer. Then one day a young woman came to see him. She was depressed, in despair, in the place he had been long before. And, as Jen told it, the priest knew then the answer to the question he'd asked years ago. He had suffered, he suddenly understood, so that he could be with this woman, so that he could help guide and heal her in her pain. "It's about death and resurrection, Firk." Jen held me while I cried. "They are real in our lives."

And, though I'm not a Christian, I saw that Jen was right. I finally had words to name something about which I'd previously had only vague intuitions: I *was* dying. Not literally of course, but spiritually, and I knew I *had* to die if I was to find a new way to live. Naming this helped me have the faith I needed to let go of old ways – compulsive, running, always trying to control things and be the "good girl." I didn't have to be on top of everything anymore. I only had to be me. I had to let go of, consciously forsake, many of the very qualities that had been highly rewarded in my schooling and in various aspects of my career. One of my students' mothers calls it "letting go into the ocean of yourself." I can truly say that letting go of all this stuff has only helped make me better at what I do, helped me become a stronger and more effective teacher and administrator.

During my depression, I felt very close to God, or whatever term one uses for the ultimate life force, and to the things that matter most to me. When I was non-functional, unable even to get out of bed in the morning, I could see more clearly what was at the center of my life. It's not unlike traveling. You strip everything away and see who you truly are. My depression made me fragile, I learned about the need and value of patience, and about how sturdy and sustaining true humility is. When we're strong and feeling confident, it's easy to believe that our ego and confidence are what keep us going, but my depression taught me that it is our ability to be humble that makes us sturdy. Since I was essentially non-functional, all that was left for me was simply *to be*. What a wonderful thing! I was given the gift of being fully present to others. I learned first-hand that in our deepest pain and sorrow, and perhaps only there, we are able to perceive and grab hold of the blessings most real in our lives. In my depression, a state of ultimate fragility, I found my greatest strength.

Six years have passed since my depression. I no longer live in a house of strangers, and I'm no longer running. I'm happily married to a wonderful man, my best friend, and every day I feel blessed to wake up beside him. Our lives feel round – not linear – although we have to remind ourselves to stay on track, not let ourselves get swept away in all the hurly-burly, forgetting the things we've worked so hard to learn. I'm always working on being more patient, humble, and clear. I pray that I do most things well and for the right reasons, and not too many things poorly and with a weak spirit. I have learned through living my life something I was never taught in school: that life is a process, round and whole, a spiral in its truest form. And that only when we let ourselves be lost can we be found.

chris

Chris, 30, grew up in Mesa, Arizona. After an abusive marriage, she moved to Asheville, North Carolina, with her new husband and children. She attended Mars Hill College and got her Masters of Social Work at the University of South Carolina while raising three children

We met while I had a fellowship at Mars Hill College. Several faculty members told me I had to meet her. I was interested in the literacy program she ran at a local women's prison and suggested we do the interview there, with some women from her group.

Chris, Lorna, a woman from the prison, and I sat in the prison library while we talked. I was reminded how vulnerability and strength can exist at the same moment. She was one of so many women who talked about the need to process emotions connected to abortion, and I wondered why so many women remain silent.

CHRIS'S STORY

I was married right after high school, had a child, divorced and then remarried at age 19 to an absolutely wonderful man. When we moved to North Carolina to get away from my former husband, I went into a deep depression for about a year. I was in my mid-twenties and I felt like I had been hit by a truck and dragged through the desert. I never left my house. I didn't have any friends. I remember days when I would sit and stare at the wall for so long my muscles ached. It was a chore to climb the stairs. I had just moved 2,000 miles away from my family. I knew no one except for a sister-in-law who drove me nuts.

A few years earlier when I left my ex-husband I had an abortion. Having the abortion went against my own moral standards, but my ex-husband was stalking me, and I knew if I had the baby I would have to return to him. I had already made the difficult break from his abuse and I couldn't go back.

So I was in this new place with my new, wonderful husband and I had to face the fact that there was a child missing from my family. I was very sad with no one to talk to about it. My husband started getting involved in the church and tried to get me to go with him. He was sensitive to my woundedness. At the time, I was a very disintegrated person and I had to find a way to integrate everything that had happened to me into something positive.

He didn't push me to get a job. He backed off and let me do what I needed to do. I stayed in the depression for quite a while. Without the use of medication, coming out of it was a gradual process. One thing that played a big role was a group we started at the church.

I was a member of a church that is very much against abortion. What could I do? Sit down at a women's luncheon and say, "Oh, by the way, I've had an abortion, what about you?" I eventually did meet a woman in my church who had had this experience and was looking for support.

We began to talk and do research on available resources. We were able to find a few Christian-oriented support groups for women who had abortions. One group we found focused on grace, mercy and forgiving yourself. It encouraged women to stop judging themselves for past decisions. When I had an abortion, I did not know I was going to run into a wonderful man, my second husband, who would have accepted that child as his own, who would love me and support me for the rest of my life. At that time I was terrified. All I knew was that if I became dependent again on my first husband, he would beat the hell out of me. God knows where I would have ended up. I learned to stop judging my past decisions based on the resources I have today.

There are a lot of hurting women who have nowhere to turn. I think both the pro-choice and pro-life movements have hurt these women because they turn abortion into a political issue. When you hear the word abortion, you don't think about the pain of women who have had one. All you see are picket signs.

I got to the point where I couldn't be quiet about having had an abortion anymore. I realized that it was a part of who I was. I wasn't who I was in spite of what I had been through, but *because* of what I had been through. My husband was the first person I told when I became pregnant with Noah, because I thought it was important for the doctors to know. His reaction helped me tell other people, because he wasn't mortified. Once I told people I thought, okay, this is my skeleton, there is nothing else to find.

When I met the woman from my church, we decided to join a group. Beginning with my own, I started speaking in local churches. It was really difficult to get up in front of people who knew me as a loving mother and say, "This is what my life is like. This is what I've done. This is what I'm going to do with it. You need to decide what you are going to do."

The day I spoke, three women from my congregation told me they had had abortions. One told me she put a child up for adoption. After that my work in this area grew and a lot of pastors asked us to speak at their churches, because they knew silence in this area was an issue. It is so taboo to discuss abortion, but I knew that even if no one else in the world could accept my abortion, I had, and that was enough.

We brought together a group of women who wanted to talk about their experiences. We met for 14 weeks. During that time we encouraged women to name the aborted baby, or to put an identity on the grief and the shattered images they had. We asked them what they saw when they pictured their babies now. Answers included: "a cold baby in a dumpster," "lying in a ditch," "I can't really see a baby," "just an arm or a leg." One woman had a recurring dream where she was going through the supermarket and as she was going down the aisle, she was picking up baby doll parts to put back together.

What I didn't realize then, is that a lot of their images were projection. They were speaking about images they had of themselves, as neglected and disintegrated. A lot of these women felt that way because they had been abandoned during their pregnancy, some of them were coerced by the man in their life to have an abortion. At the end of the group, I asked them again how they pictured their babies. For the most part, the answers were positive. "I see Jesus holding my baby with a blue blanket so I think it is a boy." "I can see my girl on a hill; she is four years old now and wearing a pink dress."

Once women talked about their experiences with other women and let out all the anger and pain, they moved through a healing process. For the most part, the women involved began with a broken self-image and ended with a more complete and positive one.

My biggest lesson through this experience is not to try to live up to anybody else's standard. We are told how to be good wives, good housekeepers, good citizens. We are not taught how to be really good to ourselves and to love ourselves. The biggest change in my life came when I gained a sense of myself.

I think a lot of being able to be depressed is environmental. In *The Handmaid's Tale*, a maiden, in order to heal goes deep into a forest and hides in a house. It is symbolic because I think women retreat into depression, subconsciously. In retrospect, while I looked shut down on the outside, there was a lot going on inside of me that I wasn't aware of.

I have a friend who went through a big depression in her twenties, but she was never allowed to fully retreat because her husband is manic-depressive and she always had to be responsive to him. Because of that, to this day she struggles with depression. She asked me, "How did you pull out of your depression and how do you have the energy that you have?" I told her I think it was because I was able to completely shut down, like going into a coma. People go into comas because their bodies are trying heal, and being awake takes energy. The body says we are going to shut down here and heal what needs to be healed. That's how I see depression. Where the broken pieces can be reassembled, that's how I became integrated.

yu-lin

Yu-lin, 29, is a first generation American born to parents who immigrated from Hong Kong. She is the oldest of three children and spent a good part of her younger years helping to raise siblings and building a community of friends and relatives. She grew up in update New York, attended Mount Holyoke College, lived in Boston for several years and currently is preparing for a several year backpacking journey through Asia and Mediterranean Europe. She has been a landscaper, neuropsychology researcher, florist, manager of a department of a homeless shelter, software specialist, waitress and more. As she talked about her past ten years, she noted, "From Alzheimer's research to landscaping to being a management systems developer—every job has been a stepping stone, regardless of the trade, to the next level of learning."

I had watched Yu-lin for a couple of years before we met for this interview. We had friends in common but knew little about each other before we sat down in her living room for this conversation. Music played across the room while she told me about her passion for dancing. As she talked about her family, her decisions and her life, she inspired me to walk with greater courage. I imagined her ready for anything and wondered how I could become that bold.

YU-LIN'S STORY

At the age of 26, I decided to join a meditation group. I had a rather tumultuous life that led up until that point—ranging from childhood incest to attempting suicide to graduating college and having very successful jobs. I had been drawn toward meditation and Eastern philosophies for quite some time. I attribute that to my Chinese heritage. A couple of friends were part of a group which made the meditation center welcoming and affirming for me.

At that time, I had been in therapy for over 4 years on and off. I was taking anti-depressants and was in an incest support group. These were activities I wanted to be involved in, especially taking the medication.

A new friend was also in the meditation group and suggested that I see the meditation teacher, Marty, for some one-on-one counseling sessions. She suggested that he would be able to offer a completely different approach than the one I was trying. My hesitation was based on going to see yet another doctor/therapist to "solve my problems."

My friend looked me in the eye and asked, "Do you want to be in the same place you are now, two years from now?"

I looked at her for a moment, looked away, looked back and answered, "No, I do not." At that point, my entire life perspective shifted. I made a decision about my life and my future. I realized that I had the *choice* to change. That I was not a victim of my past. I was a powerful, free-thinking adult. Not a survivor, but a fully-functional, open human being who had a present and a future. Such a shift was incredible and literally changed my life.

I decided that I was not going to continue several more years of therapy or take the anti-depressants. But in order to do so, I knew I had to have true inner strength and confidence. I listened to myself, rather than the babble of insecurities. If Marty could help, I was willing to try. I was willing to give myself the opportunity to change my life.

Marty welcomed seeing me as a client. We had five sessions over a couple of months. After which, I soon ended my therapy, the support group and anti-depressants. Everyone, including my therapists, saw the transition. Some predicted that the change was temporary, others had a hard time understanding it.

Marty was a catalyst for me to put my life in perspective. My openness to his technique and my ability to change my life were the formula I needed.

That was over three years ago. I have had a couple of "tune up" sessions with Marty but nothing on-going. I still attend Marty's meditation class and often try to meditate on my own as well. I have built a great network of friends in the area. Very significantly, my relationship with my family has become much closer than before.

The biggest difference is that I actively make decisions about my life. I am able to see that I always have a choice, even when I don't like what is presented. More importantly, I get to make that choice—even if is to do nothing at all.

Have I had some ups and downs? Of course. And through each down, I reached out and pulled through. Sometimes all I needed was to let some friends and family know that I was down and eventually, my mind would rev up again. I have the confidence now that I will not lose myself to my past. Now I know I am the strong, courageous, funny, compassionate and loving person I have always wanted to be. I always was, but I had forgotten that. I have a wonderful life—exactly what I *chose* for myself several years ago.

laura

After attending Davidson College, Laura, 27, took off with Up With People, a theatre group, and traveled through the U.S., Canada and Europe. A white woman from Lynchburg, Virginia, she had stayed rooted in the South. Just recently married, got a dog, and moved into a house with a bright purple door. She is an artist in everything she does. When I met her she was working at Davidson College coordinating community service activities and volunteering to draw illustrations for my workshops. Now, she is moving even further with her talents as she is in Charlotte working towards her Associate's Degree in Fine Arts at Central Piedmont Community College and working in a coffee shop.

Laura and I had worked together for several years before I interviewed her. One time we went with a small group to a retreat center to create a strategic plan. On the drive into the mountains she began talking about the struggles she was having—panic attacks, headaches, an inability to concentrate. We spent time later that day sitting quietly in a meditation center. Six months later I journeyed back to Charlotte, North Carolina, to interview her. Tape recorder in hand we sat in a restaurant and began capturing her story and learnings.

Laura reminded me how important older women can be when we are out at sea struggling to find a life raft. She also made me think about how challenging it can be to maintain perspective when our most challenging emotional issues are right in front of us and how much support we need to stay with them.

LAURA'S STORY

In my mid-twenties, I suddenly felt a huge amount of anxiety. I couldn't control it and didn't know where it was coming from. Eventually, I traced it back to the fact that when my brother was 22 and I was 12, he came back home in a severe depression. Our family never talked about it. He was always in the house and very ashamed of his condition. He wanted to hide it, which made everything awkward for the whole family. I shut a lot of people out at that time and went on automatic pilot. I developed an eating disorder.

After reading an article in a magazine one night, I said to my mom, "I think this is me." It was about anorexia. She took me to a child psychiatrist but I didn't feel comfortable talking with her. She was a threat to the world I had created for myself. She told my mom I wouldn't talk with her and that was the end of it. That was when I was 13, right after I got my period. I didn't understand what was happening to my body, but again we never talked about it. I guess that's a pattern in my family.

It all built up until the dam wouldn't hold back the water anymore. I couldn't eat. My mind was racing so I couldn't think clearly. I was nervous all the time. I was really scared and knew I couldn't go on that way. I had dealt with the eating issue a couple years before I moved to Charlotte, when I quit a job performing with a traveling group called Up With People. I came home and scratched the surface of my issues with a therapist. I knew I needed to look at my growing up and be honest with myself about some of my pain and fear. I had a huge fear of being like my brother, of living my life depressed and dependent. As a result I was always fiercely independent. I didn't want anybody to help me and didn't share any of my emotions with anyone.

It is a challenge to know your emotions, especially when you don't want them to be there. The last couple of years have been like being on the end of a whip. I had built a concept of life that was really constant. I got smacked in the head when things started to fall apart.

I got to the point where I had to tell my parents how I was feeling and ask for help. I knew I had to have the courage to stop and be with my feelings and be able to ask people for help and support.

It's been an amazing year since I've begun to take things day by day. I've come to peace with knowing that I'm a person who questions deeply and feels things deeply. It has helped me to realize that things happen for a reason. People come into your life for a reason and places exist for a reason.

Ruth, my boss, is one of the people I am lucky to have been around during the past year. She is amazing. There were times when I was a basket case at work. I cried two or three times a week, and I would go into Ruth's office and tell her how scared I was and that I didn't understand why I was thinking the things I was thinking. She has an uncanny ability to listen and made me feel I was not losing my mind. After talking to her I could cry and get back to work. She has amazing patience and insight.

The other thing that helped was writing in my journal. One night I sat and wrote about the things that scared me. I was afraid to show it to Ruth because I thought she would say I was losing my mind. The next day when I showed it to her she just smiled and said, "It's okay." Her daughter had gone through a similar crisis. Seeing that she wasn't scared by what I had written allowed me to relax a little.

I was seeing a therapist who was not really working out. She would say things that scared me. One time I went to see her with my parents and she made me sign a contract saying I would not harm myself in any way. I was shocked that she made me do that—one, in front of my parents and two, because everything I read about anxiety said you're not supposed to play with your fear. I was like, "Shit, does she think I am going to do this?" That was one of the worst things I ever had to do. I was mortified and hurt that they had to watch me do it. I quit seeing that therapist.

I then started going to a woman who does massage, visualization and meditation. Normally I would have thought that was kind of freaky, but I was getting really bad tension headaches so I went to her for a massage. She sat down and talked to me for a while. She listened to me from the inside out, to what my spirit was saying. I tried to say what was going on with me without getting upset, but my emotions surged forward. She talked about my time of life and how common anxiety and depression are for young women. She said I was basically in the middle of a mid-life crisis. I thought, "Great, I'm only 25, I don't want to deal with this."

She guided me through a meditation that released a lot of emotion. I had been angry for so long, but I loved my brother, so I never could say anything to him. During the meditation she encouraged me to get angry. It was the weirdest feeling. I felt like my body was three stories high and huge, filled with an incredible amount of anger. Then she said, "Let it out. Do what ever you can with it, but let it go." In my mind I started to shake him, and as I did, everything started to shrink. My eyes were closed, and I felt like I was huge and bloated. By the end I was beating the hell out of my brother. After a while she said, as if she were him, "I forgive you, my soul understands this. Now visualize you are hugging each other." By that point I was a wreck. Just the thought that his soul understood my anger was incredible for me.

She helped me talk through a lot of questions and fear. She taught me that you've got what you need on the inside, if you take the time to dive down and be aware of what's going on. My brother and I still don't communicate well. He is a very loving individual, gentle and caring, and though his path is very different from mine, it is also similar.

I've come to believe that if we strive to live our lives in awareness, we can begin to bring the two worlds, spiritual and human, together. My favorite quote says it well: " We are not humans on a spiritual journey, but spiritual beings on a human journey."

My brother's struggle, my family, my eating disorder and anxiety, have all brought me to an amazing place. Instead of fear, I am now filled with anticipation of what lies ahead, and I am filled with an appreciation of what already is.

Yes, I get bogged down in life's trivialities. I still have deep issues with my brother and family. When I take time to step back (meditation, journaling, nature), I see it's all a part of my human journey.

sharia

Sharia is an African-American woman in her late 20's. She has
worked on education-related issues for many years. She grew up
in Boston and now lives down South. I met her in a work context
and soon after invited her over for an interview.

Three of us sat together talking for this interview—Jenene, Sharia
and I. We sat in my old apartment and drank wine as a party for a
housemate went on downstairs. The Sunday afternoon turned
into Sunday night as each of us shared pieces of our lives and stories.

Sharia's strength and grace were an inspiration to me. Although I
had not known her long, she was quickly becoming an old friend.
Her words made me think about how many women remain silent
about early abuse and never connect to others who have also
been abused. It was one more reminder of how important it is
for women to speak their truths.

SHARIA'S STORY

What made childhood hard was that my stepfather was abusive, physically to
my mother and sexually to me. I lived with it for eight years without letting
anyone know. There are parts of my life that I don't remember at all. I always
felt like it was me against everyone else. I couldn't let anyone know my secrets
because I knew they might try to deny them. That made my relationship with
my mom very hard. Even if this man had not been sexually abusing me, he
was physically abusing her and bringing cocaine and wine into our house and
abusing himself with these substances. I now realize that my mother is a survivor too, like me. I think what I've learned out of all these things is that they
don't happen to punish you; they can strengthen you and give you the tools to
survive. I think if that abuse hadn't happened to me I wouldn't be as strong as
I am today.

I always wanted my mother to get over the abuse with me, but she doesn't even want to talk about it. I decided to prosecute my stepfather, even though it had been so long that I couldn't really remember everything. As part of the process I met two more of his victims. This man has a son with another woman who also has two daughters. For years I thought that if he was abusing me, he had to have been abusing them as well. I wondered what would make a grown man get out of a grown woman's bed to get into a child's bed?

One of the girls who was also abused by my stepfather was having a hard time with her two sons, and we started talking about our own childhood. I told her that there is a whole part of my childhood that I don't remember. As soon as I said that she started crying. I knew all these years that there was a connection between us, and that's what it was. Abuse.

Silence is what perpetuates abuse. I never told anyone because of how it made me feel. When you're seven or eight years old and an adult you're supposed to trust is doing something that you know they're not supposed to be doing, it is total confusion. Now that I'm an adult I know being sexual is supposed to feel good.

There is a right time and a wrong time to share pain like that, but I think it is important to eventually get past it all. You can't worry that you're going to ruin the family. It doesn't matter anymore. The ultimate sacrifice is to go through life with the deep, dark secret that you were abused by some man who lived in your house, to sacrifice so that everyone else can continue to live happily ever after. It is so important to realize that it's not a selfish act to bring the truth into the open. It's freeing yourself from the darkness and the sadness, to be able to come clean and be honest to the world.

I had a group of friends who asked, "Why are you prosecuting him? Sending him to jail isn't going to help him anyway." I believed that he wouldn't be able to do what he did to me to anybody else if he was locked up. He has custody of a little girl and I felt that just because he thinks she is his daughter doesn't mean he isn't going to harm her.

I feel lucky that I've been able to turn so much of my anger and negative energy into something productive. Parenting and having children means a lot to me because I see so many children who don't have any guidance. Too many kids are killing each other, selling drugs to each other, and living amid destruction. My experiences and all that I see led me to make the decision to dedicate my life to helping others who don't have the tools to make their lives better. Somewhere along the line, I decided life would be better as a survivor than a victim.

cara

Cara, originally from Newark, New Jersey, is African-American, lesbian and 28 years old. She lives with her girlfriend in Hanover, New Hampshire, where she is completing her undergraduate degree at Dartmouth.

I met her when she was giving up on school for a while at age 19. She came to Washington, D.C., to plan a conference for student activists. For the next decade we traveled in the same circles and did similar work. I always watched, hoping that some of her bravery would wear off on me if I stood close enough. I played hooky from work to meet her during the day for this interview. We hung out on her front porch and talked and once the interview was done we retreated to her living room couch to watch a movie.

Her story reminded me how much we get passed on from our families and how capable we are of moving beyond it. Cara has taken so many bold steps towards a powerful, alcohol-free life, she gave me great hope for anyone fighting addiction.

CARA'S STORY

When I was two my mother sometimes used to put beer in my bottles. My mother and stepfather have been drinking all of their lives, at least as long as I've known them. She would say, "If you love me, you'll smoke a joint with me," or "If you love me, you'll have a drink with me." That's how my addiction got started. As a result, one thing I needed to do to stop drinking and smoking was get away from my family.

When I went to college I kept up a facade that said, "Everything is fine, don't worry." Underneath that, there was a lot of terror. During my sophomore year, my last year in college, my mother and I completely parted ways. She started sending me letters telling me how much she had always hated me, and how much she didn't want me around again. I just drowned myself – I drank and slept with all of these guys to avoid facing my reality. In the beginning of the second semester things spun out of control.

I started to worry. I was running around trying to save the world, and it all landed in my stomach. I got really sick in the summer of 1994 and was in bed for about a month. That really shifted my perspective. After that I decided to get a job to make money, one that I was less personally engaged in. I've now made a conscious decision to take care of myself. Getting sick really helped a lot. I stopped smoking. I stopped most of my drinking. That happened because I hit the wall.

I still struggle with drinking because I'm an alcoholic and I've had a drinking problem most of my life. I have hurt people physically twice. One time I punched my college roommate in the face. Another time I threw a friend across the room because he wouldn't let me get to the beer. Those were really important events because they made me realize how destructive I can be, not just to myself. When you drink you feel like a one-person island and you believe you can do it as much as you want and as often as you want because you are only hurting you. When you recognize your impact on the community around you, you realize you are hurting others as well as yourself. I have been strong lately: building wonderful relationships, living in a house where drinking is not tolerated. I've stopped thinking about myself as "I" and started thinking about myself as a "we."

A good example of my living the notion of being a "we" happened with my brother Antoine a few years ago. He was going downhill fast, like one of those "walking dead." He was a completely addicted crackhead, he had lost everything he owned and was living on the street. One day my mother looked out a bus window and there he was with a homeless bum, sleeping on a bench. He had lost a lot of weight and weighed only 105 pounds. He had pockmarks all over his face.

Sometime after that he came to my mom's house. I happened to be there visiting. He had been clean for nine days. He said "Sis, this time I'm gonna do it, I'm really gonna do it." I had a six-month AA key chain that I got to mark six months of sobriety. I gave it to him. He looked at me like I was crazy and said, "Man, you got to be crazy there ain't no way in the world I'm gonna make it six months. You got to be sick." I said, "Just take it." He took it and he gave me his "one day at a time" key chain that I have today.

Two years later I went to a training in New Jersey. Antoine was in Secaucus, New Jersey, and I called him and said, "I'd love to see you." He told me, "My friend's going to give me a ride. I'm on my way." As I was waiting, I was sitting there and thinking, "I'm so stressed, I'm so stressed." And then he walks up looking like a dream. He's now well built and muscular. His face is clear, he is dressed really nice and looks like an incredibly handsome guy. He came over and gave me a big hug, and he said, "Hey Sis, how you doing? You know I love you, right?" He said, "The only thing that kept me going in rehab was the fact that you gave me that key chain. I kept looking at it and saying, okay, I can do this. I can do this."

Antoine was clean as a whistle. He admitted, "It's hard as hell. Sometimes I want to smoke. Sometimes I want a drink. Sometimes I want to smoke a joint. But I don't." We talked for a couple of hours, and it was the most powerful experience I'd had in a long time. After that I would write him and sometimes I send him some money and pictures. I was never judgmental, just really proud. He told me, "You don't know how much you helped me." And I told him, "You don't know how much you helped me." I would look down at my key chain and say no, I'm not going to do it.

It is a powerful example of how I am a "we." Although Antoine was far away, he was relying on me and I was relying on him. So I had no choice but to be a "we."

In the past couple of years I've made a real transition. I work part time, the way I want to. I live in a house where nobody drinks. I'm in a sustained relationship and I'm going back to school.

jenny

Jenny, 34, is a married youth worker and marathon runner who lives and works in Boston. For the past ten years she has been leading young people and young adults through workshops in the U.S. and as far abroad as Australia. Jenny founded and directs the Resource Center for Youth and their Allies, which assists young people to organize, and she directs Youth on Board, a youth-empowerment organization.

During my first week in Boston six years ago, I walked into a youth agency called Teen Empowerment, and a short, energetic blonde on crutches came out to greet me. I could tell immediately, by her energy, that it was Jenny. Many people had already told me she was the best youth worker in the city. We went to a cheap, greasy Chinese restaurant for lunch and by the end of it I knew I had my first friend in Boston. An ironic juxtaposition to our first meeting, we did this interview in the fanciest hotel in the city.

As she spoke she reminded me of many women I knew in college who had similar stories. She highlighted how important tools and support are in the struggle against addictions. I am lucky to know Jenny now and to be able to see that there are many women living with great strength to face diseases such as anorexia and bulimia, widespread diseases that were to close to unheard of by the general public twenty years ago.

JENNY'S STORY

Between the ages of 24 and 26, I spent two years high on Nutrasweet. I had about five diet sodas a day, and ate Crystal Light like it was going out of style. I was getting almost no other nutrients and I knew I couldn't keep living like that. I was even hospitalized a couple of times. I kept trying to fight it, but I wasn't ready to stop. I think breaking up with my boyfriend Neil helped me make the decision to take charge of my body.

I was driving out to Worcester all of the time, about 30 miles from my home in Boston. Neil would never visit me. I was giving up a major piece of my life. I remember one time something clicked. I left his house and I stopped on the

Mass. Pike at Burger King. I just sat and wrote on a pad of paper, "I'm not doing this anymore. I am not living my life around a man. What I want has to come first, and if that means feeling lonely and being lonely, then I am going to do that." So I called him up and said we needed to talk. That was the beginning of breaking up and taking charge of my life.

As women we are trained to lose ourselves and function for someone else. This plays out in a lot of ways, and for me it played out by staying in a relationship and not thinking about myself. In addition to the break up, a couple of years later I got into a terrible bicycle accident and almost lost my foot. My ankle was almost completely ripped off. In the hospital I decided that if I was going to make it out walking, I was ready to get serious about taking care of my body and taking charge of my life.

As my leg began to heal I began to exercise. I moved from running once a week before the accident to running marathons, doing triathalons and exercising almost every day. Exercising is one of the only things in the world that I can remember I am doing strictly for me. Some women have a negative connection between an eating disorder and exercising to keep them skinny, but it wasn't like that for me. I was exercising because I could remember that my body was important to me and because it felt wonderful.

As I got to know more about the patterns connected to my bulimia, I also came to realize that when I eat crazy, work too hard, and spend all my time taking care of men, I can't remember to think about myself. Through a process called reevaluation co-counseling, I was able to release a lot of stuck distress that limited my ability to put myself first and to care about my body. I had to do a lot of crying before I was able to really take myself, my body and my dreams seriously.

Along the way I got into another relationship and got married. When I got married I intentionally set up the marriage so that I say and do what I want. I did not buy into a marriage where I live for my husband, but rather *with* him. I travel and spend a lot of time with my friends. I have a good time with my husband, not because I feel I have to, but because I want to. I also married someone who challenges me to keep dreaming and breaking through limits that exist in my mind. He is someone that actively takes on sexism, and that makes a huge difference in me taking myself seriously.

On a very practical note, I learned some things about my eating patterns. I learned that I had to cut out the most addictive foods in my diet. If every time I eat sugar I have to eat 10 pieces of it then I don't ever need to eat it. I've had to convince myself that I can't have it in my body. I've asked lots of questions and learned a lot about food. I've also asked for a lot of support. I still have a locked cabinet in my house where foods I am most likely to binge on are kept. It's been helpful when friends remind me I don't want to be eating certain things.

Sometimes I cook for the week on Sunday. I have a big pot of something around all of the time. I also ask my husband Tim to help me cook. I put a lot of time into planning my meals. It's helpful when people ask me what I am going to eat for the day. I've had to remember that I can do this. It's taken a lot of determination. And I've had to rely on other people to have confidence in me when I haven't. Another thing that is connected to eating is exercise, working towards an athletic goal. I always feel better and eat better when I am exercising regularly.

I think I always wanted to take care of my body, it was just necessary to get enough hope to know it was possible. I had to ask, "Who am I living for?" I'm not living for anybody else. I needed to remember that I was really in love with my body and myself.

edith

Edith made her way from Illinois to Boston. After graduating from the University of Illinois Champagne-Urbana, she moved to work with City Year, a national service program that involves young people in community service. She is 30, white, single and about to buy her own house.

Most of this interview was conducted on a Boston city bus. This interview began over a lemon poppy seed muffin in Today's Bread, a cafe in our neighborhood of Jamaica Plain. But before long we moved from the cafe to the back of a city bus. Although we had lived together, worked together, and played together, I had never heard this story.

She got me thinking about how important friendships are when we are so far away from our families, and how critical those friendships can be when we are in need. She inspired me to think about the kind of friend I am.

EDITH'S STORY

I've always had close girlfriends I would do anything for, whom I loved, and who I felt would do the same for me, but this was never really tested. Late in my twenties, my best friend hit a severe depression and I was tested.

It had been building for a while, but there was little I could do to prevent it. Nancy had been isolating herself and didn't want help. She didn't have energy to do things because she was spending so much of it fighting how she was feeling. She thought she was hard to be around, so she was pulling back from social engagements. I tried to get her to go out or to open up about what was going on. She came at me defensively, saying, "What are you trying to do?" I told her, "I don't know. I am throwing out as many options as I can, hoping that maybe one of these times you are going to say yes. I can see that something is going on. I watch you walk into work with a look on your face that I don't think anyone should ever have. You look horrible and I'm worried about you." We had that conversation a couple of times.

Late one night her boyfriend called me and said, "Please come over. Nancy is really bad and I don't know what to do." I got up, got dressed, borrowed a car, and went to her house. She had been crying for hours, curled up on her bed, extremely distraught. Her eyes weren't clear and she wasn't making sense. When I got there John opened the door and said, "Have you ever dealt with anything like this?" And I said, "No, but I feel fine going into it." So I spent the night with her. It was the first of many where I held her, stroked her hair, and told her over and over that I loved her, that she could make it, and that I wouldn't leave her.

That night at the door I said I didn't know anything about depression. A couple of days later I was talking to my sister and I remembered I was totally wrong. I've dealt with it a lot. Both of my parents have been depressed on and off for most of my life. I had a suicidal friend in high school and two depressed college roommates. I've danced with depression myself. These experiences normalized depression for me and I quit thinking about it as something unusual.

The next day I started talking to the counseling center that we have access to through our work. I took a few days off work and found Nancy a program through the center. She went there every day for a month and started medication and therapy. It was clear that she was unable to deal with the details of her life, so I took on a lot of them. I talked to her supervisor and arranged time off, handled her email and voicemail, talked to our other friends, screened calls, brought over food at night, etc. – anything so that she could concentrate on her health. I spent a lot of time just being around so she wouldn't feel alone. I talked with her a couple times during the day, including a never-to-be-missed call before sleeping.

Nights were particularly hard for her. We spent a lot of them together. If I hadn't been there some of those nights she would have tried to kill herself. One particular night was harder than the rest, and it came after a few days that were tiring for me. We were at my house and I thought she might leave during the night to hurt or kill herself. I was so tired that I wasn't sure I would wake up and didn't know how to handle it. I couldn't think of anything better than hiding her shoes since it was winter and cold. I thought I would hear her looking for them, or that if she left she wouldn't get very far without them. I didn't tell her about that until times were much better.

The next morning I woke up before she did and called my dad, who is a minister. After my brilliance in hiding Nancy's shoes, the only other thing I could think of was to ask my dad to have his congregation pray for her. Nancy woke up and overheard part of the conversation, and was frightened that I was asking for help in that way. As willing as I was to do what was needed – it was also important that I reach out to others to support her and to support me. I kept other friends up to date and whenever I could, I asked them for help.

This was a test, but it had an easy answer. It made me think about how mothers must love their children, that it is automatic to protect your child or make any sacrifice to make their life better. I felt that way with Nancy. What I should do and could do for her was easy for me to decide. It was challenging but I would have done a lot more if it had been needed. I know now how strong a friendship can be and what I'm capable of.

depression, addiction & abuse

GUIDING QUESTIONS

- Which case study gave you new insight or made you think about some aspect of your life? How?
- What is your relationship to depression? Have you ever struggled with it? Have you ever witnessed or helped someone else deal with it?
- Do you struggle with addiction? Where have you found support for it?
- Have you been abused? If yes, have you found support for processing it?
- If you are currently in an abusive situation, what would it take for you to leave it?
- What keeps you from sharing your struggles? What are you most afraid of feeling or talking about?
- What kind of support has been most helpful to you in the past? What kind of support do you want in your life now?

EXERCISES

Make a Reach Out List

If you needed to talk to someone, who would that be? Make a list of people you can call and keep it somewhere. Pull from it when needed. If you can't think of anyone, what are some of the qualities of someone you would want to talk to? Start reaching out to people who have those qualities. Talk to people on your list when you are in a good space to let them know you may give them a call. Let them know what you need from them. Do you just need them to listen; do you need them to remind you of anything, etc.?

Write Your Story

Sit down with pen and paper and let yourself go. You don't have to know all the details and you don't ever have to show it to anyone. Just write. Write what ever you want to about your story and this struggle. What you remember, what you don't remember. Feel free to make parts of it up. This is an exercise you can do many times.

Take a Day Off

One of the things that keeps many of us from our demons is that we keep running so we never have to turn and face them. Plan a day of sitting still, resting, dancing, painting, hanging out, or doing whatever revives you. Let yourself wind down and let emotions bubble up if they need to. Find a book about the topic you are struggling with and spend some time with it.

Identify Some Resources

Even if you've never been depressed, or struggled with addiction or abuse, a good listing of resources is helpful to have when you or someone you know needs it. Ask friends or local social service agencies whom they recommend as therapists, support group leaders, etc. Get on the Internet and plug in some key word to find new resources. Talk to people who have used those resources and get their opinion.

Write a Prayer

If you believe in praying, use it. Create a blessing or prayer for yourself to help you with this struggle.

Learn Some Coping Strategies

There are many excellent books that can help in dealing with depression, addiction or abuse. Check out any library or bookstore.

Join or Start a Support Group

Whatever your struggle is, there is probably a support group that might help you with it. Many communities have support groups for individuals struggling with alcohol, drugs, overeating, being a child of an alcoholic, sexual abuse, and much else. Contact churches, social service agencies, hospitals, or city government to find out what services exist. If there isn't a support group for your struggle, consider starting one. If you are unsure about joining a support group, give it a try once to see what you think. If nothing else, it will probably be a learning experience.

Attend a Religious Service

Many people have found great strength and support from God or from religious institutions. Find a place where you feel comfortable and start attending.

relationships &
spirituality

explore

For four years I walked around Boston searching for the perfect church. I went to one church one week and a different one the next. For a while I settled into a big, primarily gay and lesbian church in downtown Boston. I almost joined because I felt so welcomed, but, I couldn't quite do it. Even though I went to services for most of three years, I never got called to serve on a committee or join a small worship group because I wasn't a member. I missed out on a lot of the community within the church.

When I got back from my trip to write this book, I decided it was time. I had to commit. I reminded myself that it did not have to be the perfect church. I knew I might change my mind the week after I joined, but I had to join. So I did. I went for a couple months to a predominately black church with my roommate. Although I struggled for a little while about being a white woman in a mostly black church, eventually I got over it. It was a church that deeply fed my soul, and a place where I felt welcomed. I loved the singing, and the preacher could preach like no preacher I had ever known. I left energized, hopeful and with a great sense of connection to the rest of the congregation. One Sunday when they asked for people to come forward for membership, I left my seat and journeyed up. Ever since, I have had a new commitment to the church.

What I've found is that by making a commitment, I am able to go deeper with my faith. It is easier to notice my lack of consistency and my impatience. And I feel more thoroughly at home in church than I have in a long time.

My lack of commitment, however, is fairly typical. Wade Clark Roof in his book, *A Generation of Seekers: The Spiritual Journeys of the Baby Boom Generation* notes:

> Baby boomers were exposed as children to their parents' religions, then rebelled. Generation Xers have been far less exposed to traditional religions. What I see with them is the search of a tourist. A pilgrim works within a faith or tradition and journeys. A tourist looks at things, tries things out, picks up something here and there, then goes on to look for more." (249)

For some, committing to a church or religious institution is the step they need to take. For others, the quest is not to find a religious institution, but a spiritual practice of some type. Claudia Horowitz, interviewee and good friend, just finished writing *A Stone's Throw: living the act of faith*. In it she talks about her development of a spiritual practice:

> My spiritual practice is an act of remembering who I am and who God is in my life. Though it is undefinable to a certain extent, I can begin to explain my practice in two ways. First, it is an ongoing awareness of the energy that pervades every living thing and every interaction between all living things. My practice is an attempt to be continually aware of this energy, the life force, that which I often call God. Second, and more specifically, my practice is the time I take every morning to be quiet and sink below the surface of my daily routine and my mind's chatter. (77)

Making commitments to relationships can be similar in some ways to the ones we make with religious institutions or spiritual practices. I've found that both types of commitments often show me where and how there is room for growth in my life. They highlight both my stronger sides, and those that need a bit of work.

Two years out of college I fell in love with a wonderful man. For several reasons, it ended four years later. Following the painful breakup I spent many hours wondering why I couldn't settle down the way I'm sure my mom would have. Was I searching for something that I would never find? Was I too scared of commitment? Had I been trained so well not to settle for too little that I would refuse to give up other parts of my life for a man?

I think many women sit with questions like these during their 20's. We are trying to define a life with meaning and joy and we know that both relationships and spirituality can play a big role in those things. As you think about your own relationships and spiritual path, listen to these stories and think about the lessons you have learned.

- Katie offers a funny depiction of the social pressures to marry before she is ready.
- The church is not only a place that supports spirituality; it also can be a major force in creating community. Tene talks about her experience with the church and the importance of being rooted during her twenties, a time of significant growth.
- Yvette decides not to get married until her late twenties, even though many around her are taking the plunge. She talks about the benefits of waiting until you are older.
- Getting married is one thing, staying married and putting your spiritual life in the center of it is a whole other thing. Dana talks about how she developed a spiritual life out of nothing, having grown up in a family where God was a bad word.
- Claudia developed a spiritual life when she realized she needed a greater strength to do the work she was trying to do. She began talking to friends and was led down a path towards meditation and yoga. Eventually she figured out how to weave together her work and her spiritual life.
- Luna, raised in the Catholic Church, rebelled and found her way to a new spirituality, rooted in the earth. She advocates following your heart, even when there are only tiny glimpses of where it might lead.

katie

About half-way through my year of interviewing women, this article appeared in my mailbox. My mom, of course, had sent it. For several years we had gone back and forth debating the need for me to get married and have babies. She thought there was something selfish to the single life.

When I got to the end of the article I was bent over in laughter. It hit a cord that was deep within me.

KATIE'S STORY

The other day, standing in the middle of the Pottery Barn store innocently looking at glass coffee tables, I glanced up at my mother and saw that her eyes were welling up with tears. "Mom, what's wrong?" I rushed over to her, alarmed. Suddenly overcome by the symbolism of table lamps and picture frames, she blurted out, "I just don't want you to spend your whole life alone."

It's hard for my mother – married at 21, pregnant at 24, divorced at 27, married again at 30 – to understand what she sees as my stubbornly prolonged singleness. Ever since I turned 25, she's been on a campaign of terror, humor and public shame to get me to settle down.

It doesn't seem to matter that I'm just doing what everyone else I know is doing. Only two of my good friends are married, and their weddings were regarded as something of an eccentricity. The rest of us exist in an ambiguous state of rented apartments, takeout dinners, and postponed futures. We all want babies, but we want them in the abstract way that children want to be ballerinas and fireman when they grow up; we want them "in a few years." The biggest commitment that a surprising number of people I know have made is to a cat.

On Sundays, my mother studies the wedding announcements in the newspaper as if looking for clues – or at least she did until recently, when she announced that she has "given up." It seems that a lot of my friends' mothers share my mother's pangs of bewilderment or envy: why aren't their successful and otherwise normal-seeming children settling down now that they are nearing 30? They don't recognize that the relationships my generation have in their twenties can be like marriages, that we are having the equivalent of our parents' first marriages without calling them that.

Could it be that lurking inside all the feminist mothers of the 1970s is a 1950s housewife who values china patterns and baby carriages above the passions of the mind? Lately I've noticed my mother dropping the word "old maid" into casual conversation. She refers to me as "the Spinster," even though, in what may be its own kind of sickness, I haven't gone 24 hours without a boyfriend since graduating from college. She buys increasingly lavish wedding presents for the children of her friends: "At least someone's procreating the species." She takes me to Tiffany, where one of her friends' daughters is registered, and shows me the tiny sterling salt shakers and glittering crystal soup tureens as if to say, "All of this could be yours."

I look at this beautiful silver haired woman gazing intently at four different shapes of spoon and have trouble recognizing my bohemian, Upper West Side mother, the one who taught me that work was essential, that having children and arranging your house beautifully was not the be-all and end-all of the female experience.

I'm beginning to think there must be a biological clock for grandmothers. My mother seems to contemplate every development in my life in terms of how it affects her grandchildren-in-progress. When I look for apartments, she worries about where they will go to school. When I mention a man's name more than three times, she thinks about whether or not he would be a good father. I think maybe my mother is planning for her immortality the way other people plan for their retirements.

My mother's aspirations have turned out to be contagious, and the problem of marrying me off has become a family sport. Last Thanksgiving, my older sister Emily said, "If you're not careful, you're going to turn into an aging femme fatale with two little Chihuahuas tucked under your arms." And my 9-year-old nephew turned to me over Domino's pizza one day and said very seriously, "Katie, maybe if you learned to cook someone would marry you." I'm starting to understand how Jane Austen's heroines feel as they reach their late twenties. I picture a life of solitude, with three cartons of coffee yogurt and a bottle of white wine staring out at me from my refrigerator. I have dreams about having a baby and giving it to my mother to raise.

Sometimes I try to argue with my mother. I use feminism and U.S. Census Bureau statistics and all sorts of manipulations of the truth. The truth, of course, is that she's right. All of Western civilization is on her side – Darwin, Freud, Martha Stewart. All I have is a wild impulse, a lingering immaturity, an overwhelming desire to stay up until three in the morning drinking margaritas with my friends or reading 900-page biographies until the sky is streaked with pink, not worrying about who is going to make breakfast or walk the dog or buy diapers, for just a little bit longer.

tene

Tene, whose story also appears in the Work chapter, spent two years after graduation as an Admissions counselor at Davidson College. Among other things, she led a support group for black women and directed a leadership module for multicultural students.

It is not suprising that she has spent much time in her life going into issues head on. There was nothing about her that showed fear about dialogue or action. She was the fourth interview in a row that opened up my eyes even wider about the lack of real dialogue between black and white women. She made me wonder what would happen if black and white women could begin some very real dialogues about our lives, our struggles and the support we can offer each other. I left our conversation and talked with many others about this topic as my journey continued.

TENE'S STORY

Going to Davidson College was the first time I was around a lot of people who had the material things I wanted to have. When I graduated I knew I wanted my children to have these things. I think subconsciously I looked for boyfriends who made money, who had a look of being connected to money. And I found one. He was an engineer who had a house, a Ford Explorer, and motorcycles. Because I didn't have these things growing up, I valued them, even though I knew they shouldn't be important.

Over time it became crystal clear to me that I was last on his list of priorities. I wanted to get married. He would say, "After I get the house." Then he got the house. Then it was, "After I get the MBA." Then he couldn't commit because he wasn't making enough money. Eventually I said, "Marriage is not about money. You think I'm going to be here when you finally want to get married. Things are fine now because I'm here if you need a pretty person to go with to a party."

Spiritually we weren't in the same place. We would talk about what might happen if I needed to move because of my career. He would be thinking, "You don't make enough money for us to move." As I thought about it, I knew I wanted to marry someone who would be willing to pick up and move for me and with me. For me, the whole idea of marriage is to get things in order together, to grow together, not just to have one person get it all together and then get married.

One time we went out and he talked nonstop for 30 minutes about his day, I finally said, "You aren't really interested in my day," and he said, "What do you mean?" I said, "For 30 minutes you've been talking nonstop about your day and even though I don't think you would ever admit it, I think you think what's happening with my life and my career is just "that thing," but to me it is really important."

It was hard to break up. I got used to having a person and a romantic relationship in my life. It highlighted for me that I was really superficial. I remember looking at other guys and thinking, they don't have as nice a body as he does, I bet he doesn't work out, his car is a wreck, etc. It took a while to get used to little things like going to the movies or out to restaurants alone. People at work were always trying to fix me up and I went through a string of funny dates. One guy's beeper went off the whole time we were at dinner. "Laquisha" was calling him. I remember thinking several times, the dating thing is just not worth it. I had a good life – I just need to accept the good with the bad. I've seen what's out there and it's not that great.

It was the first time in my life I felt really lonely, but I definitely made the right decision in breaking up. I've learned how to be by myself and I've come to appreciate gifts in people who look nothing like the kind of guy I would normally date.

I learned to do things by myself for a good two or three years. People would say, "You go to movies by yourself?" Now, I'm completely comfortable with myself whereas I used to be dependent on being with others. I've lived by myself for four years and it's going to be hard to live with someone. I love fixing up my place and having slumber parties and doing what I want to do. During this time alone I have built really solid relationships with other women who are in similar situations. I'll be excited when I get married and do "couple" things, but this is a time in my life that I'll look back on and smile, because it's fun. Sometimes I just sit in my living room and say, "I love my house, it's just mine, and I love this neighborhood." Not in a Pollyanna way, but because of the freedom.

tene, con't

Tene's story continues as she talks more about her faith and the role of church in her life.

TENE'S STORY, CON'T

My commitment to my faith has been tested a lot during my twenties. People I work with don't share the same way of being that I do, which makes me hold firm to my faith. I really have to believe in it, not just have it be something I do on Sunday. It's something that I live. My boyfriend said to me, "I don't know many 25 year-old black women who are virgins." That's a decision I made that has to do with my faith, and I think it's the best decision for me. I know myself well emotionally, and I know how hard it was to break up with my old boyfriend. I can only imagine how difficult it would have been if I had gone to another level. I want to wait until I'm married to have sex.

This is also the first time in my life that I've attended an all-black church. South Tryon Presbyterian is a small church that a friend encouraged me to attend. I've been going there since college and it has totally transformed my life. It has put me more in touch with black people than I've ever been before. I went to a white college, and Sundays are the only day that I'm in an environment where I am in the majority, where I'm not the only black.

Many of the church members are from Charlotte, went to Johnson B. Smith College there, and never left the city. Their gramma, auntie, and aunts are here. And then I come in, with my HotLanta attitude, and think I got it going on. I talk and dress differently than most of the people in the congregation. But since coming here I've learned a lot. I've learned not to be so judgmental, for example. When I first went to my church I was one of the only single people who didn't have kids. For me, I say thank God, but for most people that's just a part of life. Most of them had kids when they were 18, and they say, "You're 25 and you ain't got no kids and you're not married?" Being a part of this church has made me a more compassionate person.

My hairdresser has three kids by three different men, but whether I agree with that or not is not the issue. The point is, I love her kids, even though I wouldn't have made the decisions she's made in her life. And she loves me even though she thinks I'm a stuffy, snobby person. If I wasn't part of that church, I would not have built relationships like this one, on such an intimate level.

I've always been the bridge, both in college and after. I'm good at it because I had a real black experience and I am also in a lot of white environments. I don't think there is going to be any real dialogue until both parties are really comfortable with themselves. Most of my black friends can't believe I spend my personal time with white people. They joke with me, saying, "I work with them, but I ain't spending my personal time with them."

I made a decision that I want to marry a black man. There are just too many differences with whites. I don't want to worry about coming home sometime and saying, "Oh, the white people got on my nerves today!" Or have him say, "Black people got on my nerves today," to which I would take offense. We would have to have a pow wow about it, and I don't want always to have to talk about race. My mom's dating a white guy right now and that's cool for her, but it's not for me.

I've learned that the twenties are a really an in-between time, but also a time of major growth.

yvette

Yvette is 30 and newly married, living in Seattle after growing up in Dayton, Ohio. She identifies as African American, and is bi-racial African American/Caucasian by birth. She attended Trinity College in Washington, D.C. and got her Masters of Public Administration at the Graduate School of Public Affairs at the University of Washington.

I met her because one of my mentors suggested I call her when I was in Seattle. She was working in a community organization that helps people gain access to technology and the Internet. As I waited in the lounge of the organization I was mesmerized by brightly color posters on the wall and a steady flow of people coming in with questions.

A half an hour later we were across the street in a West African restaurant talking over a shared plate and blaring music. Her tiny frame held enormous strength and courage. She was a jolt of caffeine for my system, a great role model for women.

YVETTE'S STORY

I decided I was not going to consider getting married until my late twenties. I could date, date, date, but didn't even entertain the idea of marriage until much later in my life. This was mainly because I needed to grow and I decided to spend a lot of time on my own before it was time for me to grow with someone else. It worked out, and I'm getting married next summer, as I turn thirty. That was a hard decision to make because there is a lot of pressure on women to get married really young. I grew up in the Midwest and all of my sisters are married, which did make me feel sort of weird for a while, but waiting was the best decision that I ever made.

When I got out of college I was 21 and was in a serious relationship with a man I thought I wanted to marry. A few years later, after graduate school, the relationship ended. It was painful, but it was the best thing that could have happened to me. It made me realize I didn't want to get married yet.

There are so many things that you can't do with someone else that you can do alone. So for a while I traveled light.

It was a clear and conscious decision. It had to be, because I was being pulled in so many directions. I was always being asked, "When are you getting married? When are you having kids?" I was like, "Ahhhhh, I'm not doing it. At 24 years old I am not doing this." Even now I sometimes think, "Oh God, is it too soon?" It was like my mission statement: "I will not get married until my late twenties."

I ended up hanging out with a lot of women who are older than I am. Many of them were married and lived vicariously through my life. They would say to me, "Your life is so great, you're still single." I did have awful days, when I would say to myself, "Oh, I just need to get married"—and then I would remember that I had the rest of my life to do that. After all, I was only 20-something.

The biggest pressure to get married came from other women my age who were still single. I even gave up a friendship with a woman because it was all she could talk about. She was born the day after me and we went to high school and college together. We were like mirror images of each other, though her whole life is about the journey to marriage. Now we are no longer friends because I'm engaged and she's not and she couldn't deal with it. I would say to women in their twenties, don't get married until you're 30.

Women are so powerful—go rock your world.

dana

Dana is 30, white, married and the mother of one child living in Asheville, North Carolina. She attended William and Mary College and majored in economics.

We had been friends for years before we sat to do this interview. I was amazed at how little I knew about her and her life as she started talking. Faith had become the most important part of our relationship in the past couple of years, but I didn't know the history behind her growth of faith.

Like many in our generation, she is an example of children who grow up in homes where parents have turned from established religious institutions. She had to venture out on her own and figure out how faith would play a role in her life, her marriage and her friendships.

She made me think about how much our parents' views of religion impact our choices.

DANA'S STORY

I grew up with no religion in my home. We didn't go to church and never read the Bible. I didn't know what it was. I did visit churches with Catholic friends and temples with Jewish friends. Religion angered me. I remember going to a Catholic church and feeling I didn't belong there. It was OK for me to visit, but it was clear I wasn't one of them. I look back on that experience and know that I felt that way because it is a very ritualistic religion. If you don't know the rituals it is easy to feel self-conscious. I was a teenager at the time, which made the experience worse, because all I wanted was to fit in. One of my fondest religious memories was celebrating seder with some family friends. It was one of the few chances I had to witness another religion and feel welcomed by it.

It seemed that religion was a hard topic to talk about in my family. My mom grew up in a really strict Catholic family. My dad grew up Episcopalian. By the time I was born my parents didn't believe in organized religion anymore. My mom's family had a tragedy occur that caused them to move away from believing.

It was a weird situation, because I was always curious and upset about religion but I didn't feel it was something I could talk about. I started exploring religion a little in college, but it wasn't until I graduated that I tried to find a church and attend Bible studies. Going to a church service was terrifying because everyone else was part of the club and knew the game plan. I felt like I was wearing neon green that lit up every three seconds because I was not doing the right thing. People take their faith background for granted when they grow up with it.

Having close friends who were deeply connected to their spiriutual beliefs made me want to have God as part of my life. I remember a friend in high school who said, "God is always with me. I can always talk to Him, and I know He is taking care of things." The comfort and peace that person had was what I wanted. Once I met my husband, who has a strong, grounded faith, I said, "I want this thing that is missing."

When I was single I did a lot of searching because I was alone in a new city with a job and no friends. I had a lot of time to read the Bible, which I had never done before. It was a great experience. Eventually I decided to take a public vow declaring that I am a Christian and I believe in Jesus Christ and God. For my husband, Ted, and I, our journey with faith has been critical to our relationship.

It is so interesting to watch how people act out their spirituality and seek what they need. Some people need to be told that every single thing in the Bible is true, and they need to lead their life exactly as it says. I used to believe that because it is so reassuring. You can think, "It says this, I need to do this." But that's not where I am now. I believe God gave us the ability to think and make decisions, and I think the Bible was written by man and that the political and cultural times in which it was written had a huge influence on it. You look at how the Bible has been misused over the years when people take certain things out of it and say, for example, that God meant for slavery to occur—which is ridiculous—or to say that homosexuality is wrong. You can take anything and twist it. I doubt that's really what God wants. I believe He teaches us to love and not to judge. Judgment is His job, not mine.

My life has been so much more fulfilling with God than it was without Him. Making the decision to trust in God, which I was in the process of making for a good part of my life, has changed my life. It brought reason to many things I didn't understand before.

Making the big decisions in my life has gotten so much easier with God. When my husband and I have big decisions we pray about it or turn it over to God and see what happens. He knows what is best for us. I don't know that God is totally in control, but I think that He opens doors and then guides you in certain directions. What God brings us on a daily basis is meaning. Why am I here? What is the purpose of this? When I get really depressed, instead of thinking "I am worthless," I end up asking questions of God, like, "Why have you given me this problem? What is your purpose for me now?" It becomes a dialogue, one that will continue through my life.

claudia

Claudia is 33, single, white and a northerner who moved south to Durham, North Carolina. After graduating from the University of Pennsylvania she worked in Boston organizing students against hunger and homelessness issues. She moved to North Carolina to go to graduate school at Duke, and to stay. Currently she runs stone circles, a non-profit organization which finds unique ways to integrate faith, spiritual practice and social justice. She is the author of a recently published book, *A Stone's Throw: living the act of faith*.

Claudia was born on my birthday and is one of my best friends. We have spent days talking about God and our spiritual lives. While I was writing this book, she was writing her own about the connections between faith and social change. We sat to conduct this interview in one of my favorite neighborhood establishments, Bella Luna. We ate pizza and drank Blue Moon beer while she talked about her life.

Her story made me think about how many people develop their spiritual lives out of necessity and how little structure is around for people who aren't sure where to turn when they know they want to develop a greater spiritual life.

CLAUDIA'S STORY

For me, developing a spiritual life grew out of necessity only after I recognized how badly I needed it. A series of events in my life made me realize I wasn't as strong as I needed to be, or as I could be. I was questioning myself, my commitment to my work, my talent, and who I was.

In the summer of 1993, I was asked to participate in two national youth service events. At both events I was not strong enough to do some very hard things. As a result, I began challenging my beliefs and commitment. I did not feel that I was operating from a place of strength, and I saw that I wasn't grounded enough to do my work as effectively as I wanted.

That summer I also went to Berea, Kentucky, to visit two friends, David and Jennifer Sawyer. Their farm served me and others well as a place of refuge and growth. I remember talking to them a lot about my struggles. I was asking myself and them what I needed to be more in control of my day-to-day life, to feel happier, to make the right choices. Jennifer introduced me to the *I Ching,* one of the oldest books of Chinese wisdom, which is also used as an oracle. David gave me a specific direction, saying, "You need a spiritual practice and you have three options: pray, meditate, or read." (I've since realized there are many ways to develop a spiritual practice. At the time, though, it was probably better for me to have fewer options to choose from.)

At that point prayer for me was loaded with baggage. I had always been a big reader, but it didn't feel like a very spiritual thing to do. So, I decided to try meditating. I bought *Moon Over Water*, a book on meditation. It was the perfect choice because it was accessible to me as a beginner and it made it easy to start without feeling the pressure of doing the "right thing." I started meditating and within a month I realized it had totally changed my life.

I sat each morning for 10 to 15 minutes in a corner of my bedroom that I had set up with plants, a candle, and a couple of photos of inspirational places. Only much later did I realize that I had created an altar, something many religious traditions and spiritual practices use to draw energy and attention.

I wasn't necessarily "good" at meditation, but somehow I knew that was all right. What mattered was that I did it. Eventually it dawned on me that my life had subtly changed. Instead of days with dramatic highs and lows, like a great roller coaster, I would get to the end of the day and think, today was a pretty good day. Life had a newfound evenness to it. I noticed that when I didn't meditate my day would be a lot more scattered. I tried to do too many things at once and wasn't good to other people, or myself.

This initial experience spurred me on to set aside time on a regular basis to develop my inner life. I thought a lot about my own practice, read many books, and wrote in my journal. In part, I was avoiding graduate schoolwork, but I also knew I needed to do this exploration for my sanity. On a deeper, more intuitive level, I saw this exploration as a big piece of my path.

The summer after I finished my master's degree in public policy at Duke University, I knew I needed some time off. For three months I toured around New England, visiting friends and a couple of spiritual retreat centers. One of my stops was at Kripalu, a yoga center in western Massachusetts. Being there opened my heart and took my understanding of what it meant to lead a centered life to an entirely new level. The rest of the summer was full of new discoveries, as I became more aware of my own inner strength, and my desire to live a life more aligned with the rhythm and the voice of my spirit.

When I started thinking about how all of this was connected to the work I wanted to do, I realized I wanted to integrate this personal spiritual journey with the social change work I'd been involved in since college. Slowly, I developed the idea of starting a new organization called *stone circles*, whose mission is to find unique ways to help individuals and organizations integrate faith, spiritual practice, and social justice. I work with activists who are thinking about their faith/spiritual base and the role it plays in their life and their work.

I am interested in building organizations that function in a way that mirrors the values and beliefs of people. My work is often about creating space where interfaith dialogue and reflection can occur; for the first time, it feels as though close to 100 percent of my work is expressing who I am. And for that, I feel blessed.

luna

Luna is 31, white and bisexual. She grew up in both Florida and a suburb of Boston and got her undergraduate degree in psychology at the University of Rhode Island. As long as she has been able to walk she has been outdoors exploring. She is an avid camper, runner, and wilderness teacher. She has many passions, one of which is young people. Most of her 20's have been spent as an Outward Bound instructor on both coasts of the United States and in Texas. Currently she works to support girls' development in the Bay Area.

When I last saw her she was living in a shack on the most beautiful strip of Northern California that I've ever seen. She had recently sublet the place, complete with a mermaid painted on the wall, so she could stay in San Francisco to continue her work with a girls' leadership program and spend time with her partner. It is not surprising that when asked what she is most proud of during her 20's, her answer is that she has pushed hard for the "relationship revolution: a push to get people living in a way that prioritizes relationships between the earth and people." Our interview took place back in Boston with her roommate, Yuri, over tea and freshly baked cookies.

She reminded me how important rituals are and finding places that accept all of whoever we choose to be. It is not surprising that the end of this book culminated in a ritual that she led, helping me to bring closure to the process and celebrate the new decisions I was making about my future.

LUNA'S STORY

The Catholicism I was brought up in wasn't really accepting of difference. I have chosen a spiritual practice that accepts me completely for who I am, which means seeking it out, finding people who do it, being with them. I realized that at age 30, I'm where I want to be.

My soul was given to the Christian God the day I was born, but that God doesn't make sense to me. You got a day off in high school if you confirmed your relationship with the Christian God. There was no room for other religions. I never heard of Pagans in my town. It wasn't like I could choose. My parents, in a very caring way, wanted me to have religion in my life, but Catholicism was the only type of religion I was offered.

In high school I decided that God and the Catholic Church were not right for me in terms of my values, beliefs, and politics. The other thing that drew me away from Catholicism was being with a woman, which isn't accepted in the eyes of the Church. I also realized my power as a spiritual leader. And since women cannot be priests, it was less attractive to stay and have my leadership potential stifled.

In high school my friends and I honored nature, even though we never named it that then. We never realized it was Pagan, but when I go now and practice with Pagans we dance outside under the stars, which is what we did all through high school. Skinny-dipping is what saved me in high school. Skinny-dipping in Paganism is an important manner of cleansing. At every major event in high school we did it. On the last day of school we ran out to Nicholson Pond and went skinny-dipping. That was our religious practice. We knew that once we had done it, we were graduated.

After college I started meeting people that I was drawn to and started hearing about Paganism. I moved to the community where I live because I heard about its annual lantern parade. Though it's not officially a Pagan ceremony, it is people from the community going outside at night and celebrating by walking around a pond with lanterns, which creates a circle of light. There is something completely spiritual about that for me. I was attracted to rituals like these and the people who create them.

I met people who were interested in creating rituals around the winter and summer solstices. In my work with Outward Bound, where I travel with groups of people for weeks and months at a time, something spiritual is likely to happen. Whether people want to recognize it or not is up to them, but it does happen and it's wonderful. My Outward Bound group began with group stretches, reflection, swimming, and singing or chanting at sunrise. One day I realized that I wanted to share these things in community in my personal life, not just in my work. So I began shaping that. I just came from a weeklong witch camp where 150 people were learning about earth-based spiritual practice.

To other young women who grew up in a white, middle-class, conservative environment like me, I would say, go for what you want. Follow your heart, even if there are only tiny glimpses of what you are drawn to. Even if you are wondering why you are interested in going to an event on Friday night instead of going out with your friends, just go. Grab for anything you are feeling, even if it is outside of what you were taught to know and want and believe in. Each step will help you open to something new.

relationships & spirituality

GUIDING QUESTIONS

- Which case study gave you new insight or made you think about some aspect of your life? How?
- What do you think about marriage? What are other ways you can create long-term partnerships?
- What gets in your way of having deeper relationships?
- What is your religious background and how does it impact your life today?
- How do you cultivate your spiritual life on a daily, weekly, or monthly basis?
- If you were going to get more involved in your community, what are some ways you would do it?

EXERCISES

"Word-Storm" the Ideal and the Real

Put the word relationship up on a board or on a blank piece of paper. Then brainstorm any word that comes into your mind that relates to the *ideal* relationship. Let this go on for several minutes. When your mind seems blocked, go to another side of the board or flip to a new sheet of paper. Write the word relationship again. This time list any word that comes to your mind when you think about what is true of the relationships in your life.

Compare the two lists. What is different between your ideal and your reality? What needs to shift for you to move closer to your ideal?

Write Your Relationship Autobiography

What are the stories and lessons that provide the background of your relationship life? Where have you been hurt? Where have you been challenged to be your best self? What are the characteristics of relationships that have been destructive? What are the characteristics of relationships that have been constructive?

Chart Your Relationships

Who is in your life? Do you have an inner circle? Who are the people that are further out in your circle? Do you wish it looked different? How?

Try Out Some New Spaces

If you are searching for a new spiritual home, give yourself a couple of weeks to try out different environments and notice how you feel there. What makes a religious institution feel right or wrong? Do you need to explore nature to find God? Stretch yourself and then reflect on the experiences.

Interview Someone About Their Faith

Find someone to ask about their spiritual life. What do they believe? Why? Where do they find support for their spiritual life? What rituals do they practice and how does it play out in their daily life?

Write Your Spiritual Autobiography
- What is the history of your spiritual life?
- What is your first memory about religion or God?
- Did you participate in religious events, traditions, or rituals when you were young?
- What were crises or turning points?
- Who have been your significant spiritual leaders, mentors or teachers?
- Where are you now with your spirituality?

Try Out a Daily Practice

Take a week and try a daily practice: pray before you go to sleep, meditate 15 minutes before bed, sing for a half hour when you wake up, walk in the woods every night after work. Choose a practice that feels right for you and test it out. Be consistent, even if you feel bored—push through it. The consistency can yield great results.

Write a List of Your Spiritual Intentions

What are your intentions for this day? This week? This year? Instead of goals or resolutions, think of intentions as the things you hope you can keep focused on. For example, a spiritual intention might be to take note of your blessings more often, or to ask God for help when you are having a hard time. Write your intentions down and put them somewhere to remind you of them.

Design a Retreat Day

What would it look like if you had a whole day to focus on your spiritual life? Where would you be, what would you do, and who would be involved? Once you've designed it, consider doing it. It might be just the gift you need. You can join an organized retreat, or design one for yourself.

art, education
& adventure

explore

Twenty years ago, few women would think about taking a trip out of the country by themselves. Women with doctoral degrees were very hard to find, and far too many went unrecognized for their art. Of course, elements of sexism live on. There are many places where it is still unsafe for women to travel alone. There are still barriers that women face within educational institutions. However, it is undeniable that new doors have opened in the areas of art, education and adventure.

The twenties can be a time of major growth and expansion, a time when many women choose to go back to school, travel around the world or follow a creative dream. Less dramatically, it may be the period of life during which women take a class at a community center or plan a camping trip for the first time.

Should you take a year off after college to travel, or should you get a job and settle down? Does it make sense to follow your dream to make a film and go into debt, or get a night job and try to learn film-making on the side? What is the right time to go to graduate school?

The first adventure I took during my 20's was to travel to Mexico to work in an orphanage for a couple of months. The night before I left, I was both scared and exhilarated. I don't think I slept. I had a sense that I was on the edge of something that would stretch and mold me in ways I couldn't imagine, and I was right. One of the biggest benefits of the trip was that my confidence in myself took a leap forward. Before the trip, I had no idea that I was able to navigate my way to the Guatemalan border via a bus packed with men and chickens when I knew so little Spanish. I didn't know that when I found myself in a hostel, sick with the flu, that I would be able to reach out and get the support of German travelers in the next room. I came back more confident in my abilities. Later, when I took a solo camping trip for a week, ran the New York marathon, and moved by myself to Brooklyn, my confidence grew again. By doing things I wasn't sure I was capable of, and succeeding, I was growing my comfort zone.

I've noticed that when I want to learn something, I am more successful if I am focused and specific. So when I began this journey I decided I wanted to learn how to write, meditate, and interview. At the end, I can see that I have learned all of these things and so much more. Unexpectantly, I learned about the history of Appalachia, how to drive Oregon in a day and a half, and cool tricks to use when taking care of three children under the age of 4 for a weekend. It was all part of the journey.

Creative options for young women seem more possible than ever also. Today, role models exist in almost every possible form: people who decide they are going to do their art and work odd jobs, or work from their computers at home; people who want to go to China and have no money have found tickets from courier services for $250; women who have two children and want to go to grad school have taken distance learning courses and graduated with everyone else. The challenge is to chart a course, and to be willing to change it as needed along the way.

- Yuri realized that in her gut what she most wanted to do was to study Taiko drumming. It was the thing she was 100 percent interested in doing, so she is doing it.

- Jenene left Harvard because of financial issues and decided she would spend her year off in a self-designed graduate program learning adolescent development, interviewing, and cooking on a budget.

- Therese questions where she can find support for following her art. In the end, she decided that she had to sit and write. She realized she could learn what graduate school could teach by sheer practice.

- For most of her life, Sara thought she was headed to medical school. From one experience to the next she found herself headed out to sea.

Although it is something she struggled to do, she chose to listen to her heart and let logic stay behind at the port.

- Ruth followed the expected path by going to college, but searched to find a purpose in it. When she couldn't, she left and headed to the National Outdoor Leadership School. She shares her story of trial and retrial that led her to clarity about here educational and professional goals.

yuri

Yuri is a Japanese woman who grew up in Japan, Switzerland, and in the U.S. She attended Earlham College in Indiana and majored in Human Development before making her way to Boston to instruct Outward Bound programs for 12—13 year-old girls and to teach in an all-boys middle school. Most recently she has moved to California to follow her dreams to be a Taiko drummer with a group on the West Coast.

Our interview took place in her apartment in Jamaica Plain, Boston, with Luna, whose interview is in the last chapter. We ate a meal, sipped tea, ate cookies and shared stories about our 20's. While I had seen her drum a year before, I didn't know how much a part of her life drumming was. As she talked about it, her face lit up. It was clear that she was on the edge of a great dream in her move out west.

As she talked I was reminded of the courage and passion involved in following a dream. She made me wonder why so many of us are too scared to do it and what we give up when we don't.

YURI'S STORY

One of the major decisions I made was to study Taiko more intensively in California.

I decided to go to Japan after I had moved to Oberlin, Ohio, with my girlfriend, Wendy, and couldn't find meaningful work. While I was in Japan I decided that Oberlin wasn't the right place for me to grow. I support Wendy and would love to be with her, but I knew what the space felt like and realized it wasn't a good space for me to be in.

So I decided to come back to Boston, which had very much become a home for me. After I came back, I started working for Project Adventure. It is an organization that creates adventure-based learning programs, and I had worked for them in Japan. I took the job hoping that it would turn into something longer and different within the company. When it became clear that they weren't in the place at the time to offer me the job I wanted, I wasn't sure what I would do next.

I realized that while I was doing adventure-based work that what I really thrived on was finishing work and driving to Taiko practice. I was working up on the North Shore and I would get to the DoJo, the space where we practice, early. The group gave me the keys because they knew I would always be the first one there. I would pull out the drums and just play. It was a good time for me.

I was meeting a whole new group of people who were interested in drumming. We ended up doing a lot of gigs throughout the fall. As the fall was ending, I knew the work with Project Adventure wasn't likely to work out. I was trying to figure out what my next steps were. Feeling very transient and unsure about what I was going to do, I got a call from my friend Megan, in California. She used to play in a Taiko group in Boston and moved out to California last spring to play in a group out there. She left a message and said "Some great things are happening with Taiko out here. Call me." When I called back we had a great talk. The teacher she was studying with recently went to a competition in Japan and did really well. A major drumming company in Japan offered to sponsor her career. They were looking to start a new group and asked if I was interested. I jumped at the opportunity.

It is one of several huge leaps I've made during my twenties. I made the decision based on my gut. I'm not sure exactly what is out there or what will be there, and I don't know how it will go. But I do know that I want to continue to study Taiko. I want to study it more intensively. And no matter what happens, that's going to happen, whether this group flies or not. So I found a job as a high paying nanny to work part-time to support my drumming habits, and I'm going to go and play my heart out.

I played cello for 10 or 12 years before I played Taiko. Both connect with my love of music. Taiko also connects with my time with Outward Bound because outdoor education is all about physical and mental challenges, challenging yourself to see where your limits are and trying to overcome them. And Taiko is about that as well. It also connects with my ties to Japan.

I am all Japanese. My home life was very Japanese and through my years growing up I spent my Saturdays going to Japanese school. In some ways I don't feel American. Connecting with Taiko is an important way I continue to cultivate that connection.

In a place like Oberlin I can feel those ties to my Japanese heritage drifting away. But playing with a group in Florida I did a lot of translating and talking in Japanese and explaining the culture to other people in the group. It is something that is a part of me that is concretely related to what I am doing. In some ways spiritually as well. Playing the drums for me is really soothing and relaxing, like meditating may be for some people.

There are other things I could with 80 percent of myself, like going to graduate school, but I wanted to drum with 100 percent of myself. Graduate school will always be there after I do this. I've always made decisions not wanting to have any regrets. Maybe it will work out and maybe it won't, but I need to find out for myself. Go with the gut. Only you know what is good for you.

jenene

Jenene is 29 and an African-American living in Texas. She was raised in Austin and journeyed north to attend Harvard. After three years at Harvard she quit and spent several years working in youth organizations. She is bold and bright. As a strong advocate for the education and development of young people, she has spent many hours fundraising, developing programs and promoting innovative efforts. After returning to Harvard and graduating, she has returned to Texas to go to graduate school.

When we sat for this interview, we were in my apartment with Sharia, whose story appears in an earlier chapter. I had known Jenene well for several years with she but never shared this story. I knew many people who had to leave school mid-way through and was thankful to be learning more about how challenging it can be to return to school once someone has left.

She is another example of a woman with a great ability to imagine a new reality. She made me think about my journey to write this book as a graduate program of my own and the commitment it takes to keep moving towards an education, even amid great challenges.

JENENE'S STORY

Clearly the biggest decision I made in my twenties was to leave school. It was also one of the hardest and scariest ones to make. Harvard was never my top choice, but it was my dad's for me. When I got in, I decided I could probably make it there, and I wasn't really wedded to going anywhere else, so I went.

In the middle of my freshman year my parents had a major estrangement, and my dad and my mom didn't talk. It culminated in my parents starting divorce proceedings. In the middle of my exam period, my dad wanted me to come home and mediate a discussion with him and my brother. I didn't want to be in the middle of it, so I told him I wasn't willing to come home. He told me if I didn't come home I shouldn't bother registering for school next semester. I figured I could register as an independent student and keep going anyway.

I went to my financial aid officer and was cleared to register. I didn't find out that getting independent status was a major happening until the next semester. My next semester I worked five jobs, my grades plummeted, and I went from having no debt to having $14,000 of debt. By the end of the year if I hadn't decided to leave, Harvard would have made me go.

The first semester out of school hit me like a ton of bricks. It was the first academic year in sixteen that I wasn't in somebody's school. Even though I knew that was going to be the situation, it didn't hit me until I had friends coming back, moving into dorms, and I realized I wasn't going with them. I really didn't know what was going to happen.

I had taken a job for the summer, but I didn't have a place to live. I knew I couldn't go back home to Texas. That would have been the safest thing to do, but I had to live outside of my parents' home, financially sustaining myself to qualify for loans as an independent student. I was living on someone's couch and feeling completely displaced. I would have done anything to be back in school with my loans paid. It took a couple of months to come out of that haze, but it laid the groundwork for many major decisions that followed.

I ended up working with a youth organization, which became a completely transforming experience. It pushed me to define my own life goals, personal philosophy, and guiding principles. It was really important to the process of figuring out who I was and what was important to me.

The lesson I learned from the experience was that we all have the opportunity to design our own graduate programs anytime we want. Graduate programs for life. During those two years out of school I learned so much more than school had taught me. I learned about strategic planning, graphic design, how to get around New York on a budget, finding a house, cooking on a budget, child and adolescent development, and interviewing.

therese

Therese is 25 years old, white and living outside Washington, D.C. She grew up in Eldgewood, Maryland, before she ventured out to study theatre. After years of writing and publishing poetry, she is now painting. In her work life, she has become a specialist in organizational development.

I had met Therese just days before we sat in a small Durham restaurant for this interview. She was a good friend of several other friends of mine. During the interview I felt like I was looking into a journey which I would soon know better. I had just begun to interview and to write my own stories. She was giving me critical insight and encouragement in the writing process.

Her interview raised the issue of mentors and intergenerational connections. Even though many of us look like we know what we are doing, maybe we need a little more of a hand than we are getting. She also offered a wonderful reminder that if you want to write you have to sit and write.

THERESE'S STORY

I studied theater at a big university and was involved with lots of productions through our department there. I acted, I directed, and I stage managed. Because of my achievement in academic work outside the theater department, I was offered an opportunity to apply for a university grant to fund any project I wanted. I submitted a proposal for an original one-act theater piece to be written entirely from poetry, having no idea how I was going to write it if, by some chance, I got the award. The funding came through within a few weeks, and my friends and I were left to create something from the piles and boxes of poetry I had been writing and hiding away for years. I had never shown my work to anyone before.

The production was a sold out success. The lesbian/feminist subject matter generated campus controversy. I found myself and the work to be the subject of a running letter battle in the university newspaper. I began getting phone calls from people interested in taking the piece to other theaters. I received fan mail from people who had seen the production and been moved to ask me where they could "find my other work." I remember laughing to myself as I left the theater office that there *was* no other work. This was it. I was somehow a fake—a writer with beginner's luck.

Although I had advisors, none of them talked to me about this other part of being a perfomer. I sensed that they had vision for me, but they never talked about how to achieve it. I felt very lost. I was afraid to call people back. I was afraid to write letters. I didn't know how to handle the attention or the vulnerability that comes with putting work out in the world. I was terrified. I wish a teacher or someone had been there to guide me through that time. I needed someone to hold a vision for me and help me get there.

I think that some people's families play that role, but if you don't have that, where do you find it? Where do you find the person who says, "You are going to sit here and respond to this letter or return this phone call. It's okay. You are going to walk through this fear. Trust me on this one." I did find that kind of mentorship later in my twenties, but I didn't have it then.

After I graduated, I crashed emotionally, got sober, and took a string of jobs that I was convinced would support my illustrious, fantasy writing career. I still had no concept of what it really meant to write. I knew I wanted it somehow, knew it was a part of me, but I didn't know how to listen to myself or be alone to hear the words. I worked in an elementary school teaching theater, I did administrative work, I worked for a clothing designer, and I even worked full-time, complete with suit and pumps, with a major corporation in the human resource department. I thought all these jobs would leave me time to write "when I got home." The problem was, I was always too tired when I got home to do much of anything. I created writing spaces but never sat at the desk.

After yet another job, this time with a non-profit organization, left me exhausted with little time to write, I sat myself down and said, "Okay girl, are you going to do it or not?" I knew writing had to become a priority for me or I'd lose even more years to a working style that never made room for the writing I knew needed to be done. I moved to a summer resort town on the lower, slower shore of Delaware, found a job at a gay and lesbian bookstore and began to feel myself come to life again.

After I had been there about a year, I started thinking about going to graduate school and explored a bunch of different options. I still wasn't writing much—I figured it was something I could do in school. It dawned on me, fortunately *before* I incurred a $20,000 school debt, that what I wanted to learn was *discipline*. I was still waiting for someone else to give me permission to write, to tell me it was okay to spend premium time writing poetry, to say that yes, I was important enough to listen to. I had to take responsibility for learning whatever I needed to allow the work to happen.

With this revelation came a willingness to share my work with other people. My writer friend Bonnie was also spending the summer in Rehoboth and she suggested we meet to support each other in sending our writing out to journals and magazines. I had done that a few times, with some success, but didn't know how to go about doing it in a bigger way. After our first meeting it was clear that what I needed most to do was create more work. So I set up a schedule, creating ten drafts per month for three months, then spent the next two months editing those same drafts with feedback from Bonnie and other artists/writers I knew. This was the breakthrough I had been waiting for. Suddenly, I had all these poems – pages and pages of completed poems ready to send out. I had devoted the time to writing and, with no magic except the ultimate magic that creating is, *poems got written*. The single most important thing I have learned so far is: when we write, when we actually sit there and write the words, one after another, the piece gets written. The investment in time and energy yields reams of paper filled with words.

I continued to create new work and began to send my work out to various publications. Bonnie and I researched and read journals at a writer's center, traveling several hours to cities that had a writing center, and sending our poems to places with which we felt a connection. The whole process of gathering guidelines from the various journals, formatting to their specifications, and sending the package out yielded amazing results. Of the five places I initially sent my work to, I received four acceptances for publication. I was beginning to understand another facet of creative work: If you put it out there, somewhere, somehow, someone will respond. And this time I was ready.

I have learned a lot about having a relationship with *quiet*. I've learned about sitting alone at a desk for hours at a time. Something happens to a person when they do that. I have experienced the agony of writing empty words for days and weeks and months at a time, and then the euphoria of finally—finally – having something come together. I write every day. Something, anything, every day. Everybody works differently, but the important thing is to find our own joy in it. I build my life around this creating. My study is the most important space in my life. Sometimes it has been a large, beautiful room full of windows and light, and sometimes, like the last two years, it has been a small corner in a small room that I rent in a rather small house. The space is small, but I have done some of my biggest work here. I surround the space with pictures and inspiration, candles and feathers and words. The simple fact is that I must sit and write, and sit and write some more, the next day, and then the next, and then the day after that.

sara

Sara is 26, white and living in Port Townsend, Washington. She has been an Outward Bound instructor for many years and recently got married to a man who co-led the Outward Bound trip I was on when I met her. She went to school at the University of California at Santa Cruz and studied biology. She has been around boats for most of her adult life and it doesn't look like that will change any time soon.

We did this interview sitting on the edge of a cliff, overlooking the boat traffic in the Strait of Juan de Fuca. It had been a year since I had said good-bye to her and her soon-to-be husband Chris. We had just finished a 12 day adventure in Puget Sound—rowing, sailing, and living with 10 others on a small wooden boat. The trip had changed my life and Sara was a big part of it. I watched her strength and was inspired by it. She challenged us to push through layers of fatigue, boredom and, pain.

Her interview opened some new doors into her life for me. It made me think about how we sometimes overlook the decisions we make *not* to do something and how hard it is sometimes to turn away from the likely path. She was one more voice in the choir of women who encouraged me to follow my heart and look for openings to unexpected worlds.

SARA'S STORY

All my life I knew I didn't want to live in a city, that I had to find something I could do in a rural area. Even while going to school in Santa Cruz, I felt claustrophobic and had to get away from buildings and people to feel calm again. I looked to academics to help me develop useful skills that would make me a useful member in a rural community. Health and medicine was an area I felt I could study and be good in and was certainly something I could take wherever I would go. That is how I chose medicine: by a process of elimination. In school I was pre-med but was not passionate about it at all.

Somewhere along the line, I made the decision not to go to medical school. I had to acknowledge that I was getting off the path that I had set for myself.

I first got into boats and the ocean through the Sea Education Association, a semester-long training and research program for college students based on a boat in Woods Hole, Massachusetts. I saw information advertising the program when I was a freshman. I wasn't even a biology student, but I was interested in things connected to the water so I applied and got accepted. I put it aside for the time being and didn't do it until my junior year. By then I was pre-med, but really interested in oceanography. I decided to enroll to be around the ocean, and by the time the program was over, I didn't want to get off the ship. I didn't know if it was possible to connect these experiences to my real life once I left the deck of that ship. Within a few days I was back in school, sitting in a lecture hall wondering, if I could be back on the ship why would I want to be in a classroom? I wanted to sail, and I wanted to be back on the ocean again.

I had found something I loved doing. I thought I could eventually go to medical school and be a doctor, maybe even on a ship. I thought to myself, "Maybe I will come back to it. It's not that I can't do it ever, but right now, I want to be getting my hands wet, and throwing out lines, being physical, out there and interactive."

What I didn't know at the time was that I was going to change the direction of my life. The on-ship opportunity opened me up, and gave me enough initial education to make me want more. Since graduating, I have worked on Alcion, a schooner based in Port Townsend, Washington, and on other boats, along with instructing boat-based Outward Bound trips. Being here has opened me up to a world of opportunity to work in and around and on the water. In addition to being part of the community in this boating town, I love the opportunity to sit here on the cliffs, and look out at the sailing boats and barge traffic going by.

I still think about doing something with medicine at some point in the future. Right now I don't want to dedicate the time or money to medical school, but I have been looking at physician's assistant programs. I know that in rural areas physician's assistants do many of the same things doctors do, but they require fewer years of training. It will be interesting to see the future roll out.

I remember my friends telling me when I was in high school that I was very logical, that I needed to listen to my heart more and my brain less. Everything I did was rational and planned. I was making the right decisions for all of the right, rational reasons, but they weren't necessarily the decisions that made me happy. They didn't come from passion or even a gut reaction. So, finally, when I was in my late teens, I decided to follow that advice. I knew I needed to learn how to follow my passion more than my logic. It was the best advice I ever got.

ruth

Ruth is 29, white and living in Portland, Oregon. She grew up in Lexington, Massachusetts and attended UMASS-Amherst for awhile. After leaving school, she worked, participated in the National Outdoor Leadership School and then headed out west to go to school again. After a couple of attempts she has finally graduated from Reid College and is working toward a degree in nursing.

I arrived at her house after 24 hours of driving around the state of Oregon in a rental car by. I had met her brother in Port Townsend after interviewing Sara. He offered to take me back to Seattle. Along the route we talked about the book and he insisted that I go to Portland and interview his sister. Forty-eight hours later I was sitting in her back yard under a giant tree sipping iced tea and listening to Ruth's life.

She made me think about how much persistence is needed to follow your path and how many roadblocks can get in the way. She also reminded me that it's not the end of the world if you do something different from the thing people expect you to do.

RUTH'S STORY

When I graduated from high school I didn't really want to go to college. The Lexington schools are excellent public schools, and everyone is expected to go to a four-year college. Most students in the honors classes are expected to go to ivy leagues. I had a really rough time in high school; I wasn't focused academically, to say the least. I had no idea what college was all about and was rebelling against the idea that I should go without having an understanding of what it could do for me. Somehow I was convinced to apply to a couple of places, and ended up going to the University of Massachusetts, Amherst, because I got a scholarship.

I was having problems with my parents at the time, and they would threaten to not send me to college, which is sort of what I wanted, but at the same time, I wanted to get away. With an edge of resistance, I decided I'd just go to

UMASS, and then they wouldn't have to pay for anything. Once there I got involved in a program called the Inquiry Program, which is a college within a college. It was a series of seminars, including an introduction to the arts, social sciences and sciences. At the end there was a seminar in which we talked about all we had learned and what our next steps would be.

It was a great program, but at the end, I still didn't know what I should do with my life. I was taking classes because they were interesting, thinking, "Oh maybe I will do something like philosophy," and then hating it. I dropped out after a year and a half. When I left school, my parents saw that I was in a major depression. They brought up the idea of going to the National Outdoor Leadership School (NOLS) to spark my self-confidence. I didn't really know what I was getting into, but I agreed. It is one of those things that when you show up you say, "Oh my God, what am I doing here?"

At various times in my life I have come to a place where I see that I can either continue drowning in a pool of awfulness or I can leap towards something for which there is no reasonable explanation. The Leadership School seemed like a positive leap into the unknown. I figured that by doing it I would learn a lot about myself.

NOLS is one of those experiences that is what you make of it. Eighteen of us were together for three months of skiing, climbing, and rafting. I discovered that I can have adventures, explore, and survive without taking a shower for a month. I also realized that although I didn't like some things, I could do them if I had to. I learned a lot about making the best of a situation. For me it was a time to slow down and look around and realize that I didn't need to have all of this hyperactive over-analysis of everything. For the first time in my life, I didn't have a book, so I started keeping a journal, something I hadn't done before. I discovered I could break out of my patterns much more easily that I thought I could. I could decide that today, instead of complaining about how cold it is and how the food sucks, I'm just going to wake up and look at the trees. Or if I just walk home a different way I will see all kinds of things I haven't seen before. And if I stop myself from thinking all the time about whatever is going on, my perspective will change suddenly.

That was the first time I had really taken advantage of being some place where all I had to do was get up, walk or ski or whatever, make meals, and go to bed. It sets your priorities in much better order. You don't care what you look like, or what other people think about what you look like. All of that doesn't exist. You are simply there, enjoying the people. Over three months you get into some serious disagreements with people, but you also learn how to work them out so you can live and function together, because you have to. That is a really good lesson, because people often don't do that. They think that because the world is such a big place, they can get away with not working out disagreements.

I think people have core characteristics, and one of the things that I've realized about myself is that I can survive. I can keep going and do whatever I have to, and I'm not going to fall apart. And even if I do, it is not going be forever. There are plenty of people who have much worse lives and experiences. However, the point is not to compare and say I'm so much better off or they are so much worse off, but that this is life; things happen. You can either let them stop you, or you can roll with them. One of the neat things about studying biology is that you realize we are really insignificant in the whole scheme of things. Yeah, personal pain and suffering and heartache matter, but in evolutionary time they aren't really important.

After the National Outdoor Leadership School I went back to college for lack of anything better to do, and dropped out again after a semester. I lived with my parents for a while and had a job at a Boston law firm. I spent a lot of time by myself, and I realized I really wanted to go back to school. I realized that I didn't want to stay forever in a job that pays $12 an hour, or maybe someday $14. It's boring work and doesn't get you anywhere. I want to travel eventually, and I want to have a skill to take with me.

When I decided to go to Reid College in Portland, Oregon, I wanted to be challenged intellectually and surrounded by people who cared about what they were learning. I've always been an avid reader and caught a lot of flack from people around me for having my nose in a book all of the time. I wanted to go someplace where that didn't matter anymore, or where that might actually be a good thing. I went to Reid for three years and made it all the way to my senior thesis, but didn't manage to finish for a variety of reasons. I came really close to graduating and didn't do it. But at least I liked Portland a lot.

I was 24 by then and decided to stay here. I did temp work as a secretary to support myself. One of the temp jobs offered me a full-time job, so I've been doing that for the past two and a half years. I'm getting money together to go back to school for my last year.

I have decided that I want to go to nursing school, to be a nurse practitioner and do community health work. I am really interested in infectious and sexually transmitted diseases. As a nurse practitioner there is a lot opportunity for travel, and it pays pretty well. It also allows me to give back a lot, which is really important to me.

I feel blessed with a curious mind, but it was given a lot of free reign and no direction. I missed getting that direction. I could study, but I also needed mentors and role models. I still do. One of the professors at UMASS, John Stone Campbell, was my tutor for a while, and he was the first person to play that role for me. I didn't recognize it at the time, but now I can look back and say, "Yeah, he managed to play that role." He encouraged me to follow what I wanted to do, saying, "If you want to drop out of school, nothing is stopping you. It's not a bad thing. You won't die, and it's not the end of the world." Now I know it wasn't. At least now I know why I am here and what I'm trying to get out of it.

art, education & adventure

GUIDING QUESTIONS

- Which case study gave you new insight or made you think about some aspect of your life? How?
- What do remember about being creative when you were young?
- If you could spend the day creating now, what would you do?
- What are significant learning experiences you've had in the past? Who have been significant teachers?
- If you were designing you own year of study, what do you want to learn?
- What experience, credentials, or skills do you want and why?
- What environment supports your learning? What environments limit your learning?
- If you could do anything and go anywhere, what would you do and where would you go?

EXERCISES

Paint Your Creative History

Let yourself get sloppy as you dive into painting some of the pieces of your creative history. When you were young did you draw, paint, sing, perform? What else did you do? Who were your teachers in this area? Are there periods of your life when you have not been connected to your creativity? Where are you with your creativity now?

Put Yourself Around Creative People

There is nothing quite like walking into a wildly creative space. Inspiration sings out loudly. People who have tapped into their creative sides can be a major source of inspiration to others. Find some and spend some time with them.

Create a Creative Space

Is there a place in your home where you could set aside some creative tools or ingredients (fun paper, tape, glue, scissors, glitter, old furniture, etc.) to remind you to create? A place you can visit every couple of days to keep your creative juices going? Take some time to make the space the way you want it. Decorate it, paint quotes on the wall, or set it up in a way that inspires you to think differently.

Try a Discipline for a Week

Writers have to write and dancers need to dance. Whatever art form inspires you, take some time and do it. Set yourself a goal for a week. For example, take a week and write for 30 minutes every day when you wake up.

Identify a Creative Ally

Part of the challenge in being creative is that it can be isolating. Break out of the isolation by identifying someone who you can talk to about your work, share thoughts with and get tangible support from. You may even want to set up a regular check-in with this person to talk about highlights and challenges of the week. Set up creative dates with them.

Design Your Own Educational Program

Who is teaching? What are the subjects? What are you learning? Map out a whole schedule and then step back and take a look at where you might have an experience similar to the one you've mapped out? Is it in a traditional educational setting or somewhere else? What do you need to do to work toward it? What is a plan for trying to reach your educational goals?

Write Your Education Autobiography

What is your history with education? Where have you learned well, where have you struggled with learning? Who are the significant teachers? What are the environments that really nurtured your development?

Create an Education Budget

One of the major things that gets in the way of education is money. Make some phone calls and create a budget for what it would cost for you to get more education. Begin mapping out where and how you can get this money. Do you need to apply for a grant? Start putting away a little money every week? Ask a friend or relative to support you? Don't let this stop you; you need to take the time and be strategic about it. Apply for scholarships and ask for support.

just lessons

explore

writing a book

Two months into my journey I was on my way back to mainland Washington State when the ferry I was on stopped at an island in the Puget Sound for lunch. I was tired of being around people and fairly broke so I did what I usually do when I am in that state—I headed for a book store. They are the best places to find quiet and enjoyment that doesn't cost any money. I was walking around picking up enticing titles and opening to random pages for a few minutes until I was ready for the next book. In the corner of my eye a light blue covered book caught my glance. Alice Walker's name was in big bold print across the bottom of the book. The title read, *The Same River Twice: Honoring the Difficult.* As I dove into a couple of paragraphs I knew that I had to have it. The voice she was speaking with was so honest and the topic so relevant to my thoughts at that moment. As I flipped to the front of the book, the introductory quote jumped out at me. It read:

> Once we enter (the labyrinth), ordinary time and distance are immaterial, we are in the midst of a ritual and a journey where transformation is possible, we do not know how far away or close we are to the center where meaning can be found until we are there; the way back is not obvious and we have no way of knowing as we emerge how or when we will take the experience back into the world until we do."
> —Jean Shinoda Bolen, *Crossing to Avalon*

There was something about these words that drew me towards the book. On a deeper level I knew that I had entered a labyrinth, a journey of sorts into the unknown, when I decided to write this book. I knew I was going to be changed by the process. In the final stage, I see that I have learned many more lessons than I could ever have imagined. Here are a few of them.

I SHOULD HAVE LISTENED TO BILLY SHORE.

When I set out to write, Billy Shore was one of the few people I knew who had written a book. He is the founder of a very successful non-profit organization, Share our Strength and author of *Revolutions of the Heart* and most recently, *The Cathedral Within*.

I took the train to D.C. to talk to him about what he learned from writing his book. As I sat across from him at his desk in his non-profit office, he told me, "Don't tell anyone you are writing a book. Call it a project, call it an article. Just don't call it a book because you never know what will happen." Along with that advice he offered great encouragement and an open door for further questions down the road. I walked out of his office dancing on top of inspiration and more committed that ever to writing a book. Immediately I started telling people about my plans.

A year into the project I began to understand his wisdom. Writing a book is a mysterious process that leads and directs you. There were many moments when this book was an article, a film or a short photocopied Christmas present for friends. The fact that I had told people that I was writing a book put an additional, unnecessary pressure on me. It also gave everyone I knew permission to ask me questions I usually didn't want to answer.

There I am at the ice cream store escaping my computer for an hour, hating everything about the book and a very distant friend sees me. They come over and start the interview. "So, how is the book going?" "Do you have a publisher?" "When are you going to be done?" By the end of the interaction I'm ready to shove my mint chocolate chip cone down the person's throat. What I really want to say is, "The book sucks. I hope I go home and burn it. And no, I don't have a publisher. I have 6 rejection slips though, would you like to see them?" Instead, I answer all of the questions very politely and go my way.

Letting go of knowing has been a great lesson. I have gotten much more comfortable telling people, "I don't know when the book is coming out. I'm not sure where it will be sold. I'm just taking it all one day at a time." I have been trained so well to hype it up, proclaim my security, and know all the answers. Taking a step back in this direction has enabled me to relax more into each moment and allow this process to lead me. Now I know, I should have listened to Billy Shore.

SUPPORT SHOWS UP

I used to read self-help books that talked about following your heart and find-ing the universe just lines up to support you, and laugh. I thought it was corny. I have to admit, I am now a believer.

One day when I was in the hills of North Carolina I got an awful toothache. I could barely move my jaw and my head pounded non-stop for several days. I started looking for a dentist in the area. I got a few names and started calling. One after another dentist's receptionists told me they either could take no more new patients, or that they had an opening, but not until three weeks from now. The third night of pain, I spent on the phone crying with my sister.

Feeling desperate the next day I asked another friend what I might do. He suggested a local health clinic that helps poor people. When I called them, they said I could come in two days, but they only did extractions. I'd have to be willing to loose the tooth. That was the final straw. I hung up the phone, went back to my dorm room and began to question everything about this crazy trip—the financial pressure, the leaving home, the being alone and the writing. Feeling completely depleted and sorry for myself I ventured out to my friend's office for one last round of suggestions. As I entered the door he met me with a little yellow post-it in his hand. On it was the name of his cousin, a dentist, who lived 45 minutes down the road, who could see me at 7:30 a.m. the next day. Grace happened at last.

Things like this happened again and again and again during this journey. When I needed a car, a friend offered hers for three months in return for babysitting. When I decided to move to New York, within a day I had keys to an afford-able apartment in the heart of Brooklyn. When I was sure I couldn't finish the final edits by myself, a friend volunteered to give up her Monday nights dur-ing the summer to help.

What I've learned about all of this is that if I follow my heart, support shows up.

CREATIVITY AND CRAZYMAKING ARE CONNECTED

In Julia Cameron's book, *The Artist's Way*, she talks about "blocked creatives," people who do not have an outlet for their creativity who create busyness and craziness all around them because they are not channeled. They surround themselves with other "crazymakers", whose lives are always in chaos and crisis. She notes:

> Trusting our creativity is new behavior for many of us. It may feel quite threatening initially, not only to us but also to our intimates. We may feel-and look-erratic. This erraticism is a normal part of getting unstuck, pulling free from the muck that has blocked us. It is important to remember that at first flush, going sane feels just like going crazy. (p.41)

As I read her book during this year I noticed how much I have been a blocked creative. I began to see that in my dips into depression or mania, I had temporarily stopped writing, or making quilts or dancing. My creativity was temporarily trapped and I forgot to notice. I also began looking around and noticing how much of a caretaker I am and how I have a lot of "crazymakers" in my life that keep me away from creative expression.

There is something very powerful about creative energy. When I was up in the hills of North Carolina writing for six to eight hours a day there were times when I only needed four hours of sleep each night. There was energy pulsing through my body that had the power of the Mississippi after the spring melt down. I didn't always know what to do with it. I danced around my room a lot. I did yoga and ran almost every day. And I often considered getting drunk and having sex. When the energy was grounded, it moved me to a deeper, more centered place within myself. When ungrounded, it spun me out.

I spent a lot of the year playing around with watching and trying to contain this energy. As I watched it became clearer and clearer that there is a direct connection between creativity and crazyness. To feel balanced and sane, I've got to have consistent outlets for my creativity.

MY PATH IS MY PATH

As I sat in front of Gretchen to interview her in the back room of her Internet cafe, I wanted her life. I wanted her creative energy, her lifestyle, and her courage. I listened as well as I could, got up from the interview and spent the rest of the day wondering around Seattle eating junk food and feeling depressed. Why is it that we can't have other people's lives?

As I grow more comfortable with who I am, I am continually reminded that the only life that I need to worry about is my own. The game of self-pity and envy is full of loss and wasted time. I've got my struggles and it is no doubt that Gretchen has hers. Who knows, maybe she sat through our interview wishing that she had my life. What matters is that I live my life in the most authentic, glorious way possible. I get to face my struggles, have my glory moments and learn the lessons that have been set up for me to learn in this lifetime.

At the very end of the editing for this book I hated life. I had been somewhat depressed all summer by the transition back into a 9-5 job and a radical disconnection from writing. I finally melted down at my new job, got in the car and headed out of town. First I visited my mom who for one of the first times in my life said all the right things. She listened for an hour as I talked about how hard my summer had been. Then she agreed that I was in a very difficult situation. To top it off she reminded me that there are times when we just need to turn to God and ask for some help.

I got in the car the next morning and traveled for 5 hours listening to a book on tape, The Life of Happiness, by the Dali Lama. It was the spiritual retreat I needed, but couldn't sit still to attend. There was something ironic and wonderful about traveling 200 miles while listening to a tape about sitting still. When I arrived at my god son's house I was greeted with hugs and tears of joy. I was coming home to be reminded of my path and my strength. It was exactly what I needed.

Two days after I got home I received a little scrap of paper in the mail from one of the friends I visited. It was the perfect reminder. It read:

> There is no such thing as a problem without a gift for you in its hands. You seek problems because you need their gifts.
>
> —Richard Bach, Illusions

This journey was a great one. Filled with problems and filled with enormous gifts. Through it I learned once again that all I can do is walk my own path—as well as I can figure it out.

searching
for meaning

If what I have witnessed in my life and in the writing of this book is true, many of us are searching for meaning and feeling disconnected. Suppose we are out of sync. Perhaps that there is a real crisis of meaning going on for many young adults, and a yearning for more connected and principled lives.

As I sat down at the end of this journey to look at what I've learned about creating meaning, this is what I found.

SLOW DOWN

The other day I was running errands around town. I was in a rush to get home and do some writing. Angry at not getting enough done with my day, I wasn't really paying much attention to anything. After I bought some coffee, I put it on my car seat and ran into the grocery store to buy some milk. I came out, swung the car door open and sat down right on top of the cup—spraying the brown, hot liquid all over the seat. After I yelled at myself and stuffed a sweatshirt on the seat to keep my butt from getting soaked, I stopped. I told myself that the spill must have happened for a reason. Someone wanted me to slow down. I took a few good breaths, laughed out loud at myself and then drove out of the parking lot smiling at the drivers next to me and singing all the way home. I had been jolted into remembering that there are more important things in life than getting all my errands done.

When I was writing in the hills of North Carolina, life got very, very slow. Each day I would rise, run, write for a couple of hours, have a meal and get back to writing. Everything I did, I did slowly. When the phone rang, which was about twice a day, I put down everything I was doing and did nothing but talk on the phone. When I went to lunch, all I did was go to lunch. I didn't try to run four errands and have three conversations on my way to lunch. I just walked slowly across campus, got my food from the cafeteria line and sat down with faculty members to eat. I found that life got very meaningful, very fast. One conversation at lunch could keep me thinking for many hours. A simple conversation about almost anything helped me feel connected, usually offered me some humor, and regularly reminded me how much I love people.

As I've settled back in Boston, it's been more difficult to slow down, but it is still possible. I do a sitting meditation with a few friends most mornings. At work, I will get up from my desk and walk to a nearby church and sit in the pew for 10 minutes to slow down my pace. Susan, a friend of mine, hung a bell in her car that rings when she makes quick movements to remind her to slow down.

Slowing down and noticing what really matters has been one of the simplest ways I've created more meaning in my life. Once I'm centered, it is easier to choose priorities and to sacrifice for them. That sacrifice has made my choices all the more worthwhile.

FIND A MENTOR

During my first week living in Boston, I traveled over the Charles River to the office of Mel King, a well-known community activist and educator at MIT. I had met him once before and read a book he had written several years back about community organizing. I knew that he was a person I wanted to learn from in Boston. Over a cup of tea I described the new organization I wanted to start. He listened, nodding intently and asking hard, targeted questions every few minutes. At the end of the conversation, he asked, "What do you want from me?" I mustered up my boldness and responded, "I want to have a conversation like this once a week." After a pause that has become remarkably familiar, he said, "Sure."

I left the meeting, got on my bike and a big smile broke out on my face. I couldn't believe that I actually asked for that, and I couldn't believe that he agreed to it. What I didn't know then was that seven years later we would still be meeting for tea and conversations about my life and work. While the conversations have changed over time, the consistent support has been such an incredible blessing. I've always talked to him before I've quit a job or taken a new one. And I've always gone to him when I was really struggling with an issue I knew was too big for me to handle alone. In return, our relationship has become very mutual. He asks me for help when he needs it, and often our conversations are about life in general rather than about my work and needs.

What I have loved about the relationship is having someone around who has been where I have been, and is still standing. His pace is slower, so I slow down when I am with him. His view of community change is much more long-term, so I get less urgent when we meet. He is obviously committed to me and my growth as a person, and I can't describe the impact that that has had on me. I can't imagine the past seven years without it. I'm not the only one who has had an experience like that. Holly, who I interviewed in Seattle reported, "Getting mentors is so important. I've been amazed at what women can do with a little encouragement."

More than anything, a mentor can connect us to the wisdom of our elders that many of us have become disconnected from.

TAKE A STAND

Over a salmon dinner just weeks before this book went to the printer, I had a conversation with two friends, Tulaine and Theresa. We were talking about community change and the lack of it in our city. At one point, Theresa put down her fork and said, "We have to stop waiting. We're all doing it. It's as though we are waiting for someone to come forth and lead us or for the perfect situation to arise." While I fought back for a moment in the conversation, I tried to convince them that I, myself, was not waiting. Tulaine completely agreed with Theresa. "You're right. We are waiting." Eventually, I came around to my more humbler self and realized that I too was waiting. I was waiting for a group of people around me to all agree on what is wrong with the world and in a unified voice, to speak it. I was waiting for the perfect team to start a youth center and the perfect partner to help care for foster children.

Taking a stand forces you to declare what is important. You can't be lukewarm about taking a stand because often, you have to back it up. Maybe that is why it is so scary at times.

What I remembered a day later is that taking a stand begins with a baby step. I stopped by the office of a local political leader and got a bumper sticker. Already I felt a little better. Then I sat down to write the first chapter in this book, which I had been avoiding for weeks. I was sure that I would say something that would offend someone, or write it wrong. Gradually I let go of perfection and decided to stop waiting. Maybe there were will bigger and bolder steps that come next. All I know is that the only way to learn how to take a stand, is by taking a stand—even if it is a baby step.

JOIN A GIRL GANG

When I finished the first draft of this book, I decided to throw myself a party. I sent out invitations, ordered food, and lined up women readers. The week before the party I went to a local diner and wrote a short monologue about the process of writing the book. The title, which sprung up after my grilled cheese arrived on my table, became, "Why I joined a girl gang." It was the perfect title because it captured the essence of my experience. I had opened myself up and been vulnerable to meet and be changed by women all over the country. Women who are different from me, but all share a similar courage and honesty.

These women became my gang as they cheered me on, told me their stories, and challenged my process. They were right there when things got rough. Some of them sent me notes of encouragement and others spent late nights with me at Kinko's. Others were imaginary. They were female vocalists and writers who I imagined were working as hard as I was to follow a dream, be disciplined and offer something of themselves to the world.

What I realized through this gang is that giving and receiving support is one of the most important and sometimes the most difficult steps we can take toward having more connected and fulfilling lives. When I was feeling terrible, if I could get up the courage to knock on my roommate's door and to tell her how badly I felt, my isolation crumbled right in front of me. When I answered the phone and it was a friend asking for a reminder that her film was not ridiculous, I remembered that my life has a lot of purpose.

A crisis of meaning can be the best time to begin giving and getting new support. Tene, an interviewee who talked about the connections that grew out of a tough break-up described, "During this time I have built the most solid relationships with other women who are in similar situations." One thing I know is that we are at a crossroads. Too many people are suffering and too many people are in denial. We can continue to act in isolation and put up walls around ourselves, or we can dare to notice the power and possibility in our connections.

I think it's time for all of us to form a giant gang.

bibliography

Barnett, Rosalinda and Caryl Rivers. *She Works/He Works: How Two-Income Families Are Happier, Healthier and Better Off.* (Harper: San Francisco) 1998.

Cameron, Julie. *The Artist's Way.* (Penguin Putnam Inc.: New York) 1992.

Horowitz, Claudia. *A Stone's Throw: living the act of faith.* (Stone Circles: Durham, North Carolina) 1999.

O'Connor, Richard. *Undoing Depression: What Therapy Doesn't Teach You and Meditation Can't Give You.* (Little Brown: New York) 1997.

Rape, Abuse & Incest National Network. RAINN Rape Facts. Internet. Available: http://feminist.com/rainn.htm

Roof, Wade Clark. A Generation of Seekers: The Spiritual Journeys of the Baby Boom Generation. (Harper: San Francisco) 1993.

Sheehy, Gail. *New Passages: Mapping Your Life Across Time.* (Ballantine Books: New York) 1995.

Sheehy, Gail. *Passages: Predictable Crises of Adult Life.* (Bantam/E.P. Dutton and Company: New York) 1977.

Small Business Association. Statistics on Women's Business Ownership. Internet. Available: www.sba.gov/sbainfo/bcwbo/stats.txt

Toffler, Alvin. *Future Shock.* (Bantam/Random House: New York) 1971.

Trebilcock, Bob. "Why Women Drink." *Ladies Home Journal*. January, 1998:
    p.66-68.

Walker, Alice. *The Same River Twice: Honoring the Difficult.*
    (Scribner: New York) 1996.